If I Knew Then
What I Know Now

The Clarity that Comes with
Cancer and Age

Carol Ann Cole

Pottersfield Press, Lawrencetown Beach, Nova Scotia, Canada

Library and Archives Canada Cataloguing in Publication

Cole, Carol Ann
    If I knew then what I know now : the clarity that comes with cancer and age / Carol Ann Cole.

ISBN 978-1-897426-12-8

1. Cole, Carol Ann. 2. Breast–Cancer–Patients–Canada–Biography.
3. Depressed persons–Canada–Biography. 4. Comfort Heart Initiative.
I. Title.

RC280.B8C632 2009   362.196'994490092   C2009-902700-3

Cover design by Gail LeBlanc
Front cover photo courtesy of *The Chronicle-Journal*, Thunder Bay, Ontario, and photographer Sandi Krasowski
Back cover photo courtesy of photographer Sue Mills

Pottersfield Press acknowledges the financial support of the Government of Canada through the Book Publishing Industry Development Program for our publishing activities. We also acknowledge the ongoing support of the Canada Council for the Arts, which last year invested $20.1 million in writing and publishing throughout Canada. We also thank the Province of Nova Scotia for its support through the Department of Tourism, Culture and Heritage.

Pottersfield Press
83 Leslie Road
East Lawrencetown, Nova Scotia, Canada, B2Z 1P8
Website: www.pottersfieldpress.com
To order, phone toll-free 1-800-NIMBUS9 (1-800-646-2879)
Printed in Canada

The Canada Council   Le Conseil des Arts
    for the Arts   du Canada

NOVA SCOTIA
Tourism, Culture and Heritage

Canada

*This book is dedicated to
the strong women in my family
who give me strength and hope*

*My sisters –
Lois Young
Lorraine Rosenal
Connie Dea*

*The next generation –
Tracey Scott
Natalie Mayne
Dawn Marie Balisky*

*And the next generation –
Courtney Mayne*

Contents

Acknowledgements

A very sincere thank you to my family and friends who have stood by me one more time watching me move into my writer's mode. Thank you for understanding me as well as you do, for loving me and for your help whenever I ask. I realize that lending support as I worked on my third book may be more than my family bargained for and that makes me appreciate you even more.

In addition to my own story, *If I Knew Then What I Know Now* includes heartfelt stories written by others. I appreciate all that you have shared and I love you for opening your heart as you have within these pages. I hesitate to name names because I fear I might forget someone, but I do want to thank J.C. Legault from the bottom of my heart. I realize it was not easy for you to put your mental illness and survival history on paper. I am very proud of you and I know your story will help others.

To the caring, strong and powerful team at Mount Sinai Hospital in Toronto who looked after me so well through my breast cancer recurrence in 2008 and in particular to surgical oncologist Dr. Wey Liang Leong, oncologist Dr. Martin Blackstein and Family Physician-in-Chief Dr. David Tannenbaum, thank you so much. You are part of my story.

Mount Sinai was my hospital in 1992 when I faced cancer for the first time, and it seemed that I was in the warm embrace of someone who knew me well when I found myself facing cancer again. I have written in detail about my experience and often took precious moments during an appointment with one of my doctors to talk about my book. Thank you for letting me do that. Any attempt to make light of my cancer situation from mammogram to full recovery is mine alone – humour sometimes helps me through the dark hours. Any mistakes in interpreting medical language are also mine alone.

Thank you to every holder of the heart – all 230,000 of you! I am so proud to share some of your Comfort Heart stories here and I appreciate your continued support for my fundraiser.

Because there is so much more to me than being a cancer survivor, I am very grateful to so many people who have booked me for keynotes and workshops at your company conferences since Colemind was formed in 1999. It is true that cancer often comes up during our conversations, but I am thrilled that most often it is my life's experiences in corporate Canada that you tuck away in your memory bank for your own use back at the office and in your personal life. I am hopeful that you will find *If I Knew Then What I Know Now* as useful, educational and informative as you have found my other books. Thank you for your continued support.

To Lesley Choyce and his Pottersfield Press team, Julia Swan and Peggy Amirault, thank you for helping me bring this book to life. You have encouraged me to continue to write from the heart and have allowed me to tell my story in my own way. You are a pleasure to work with and I have learned so much from you. I consider it a gift to work with each of you once again.

A very big thank you to all of you who have taken time to contact me and let me know what you think of my books. It has been a real pleasure to hear from you and to meet you at book signings and on other travels. It is all very humbling. You can reach me anytime at www.carolanncole.com.

Introduction

*M*y childhood neighbours from Wilmot, Nova Scotia, arrived in Toronto to help me celebrate my birthday. Their last names may have changed but they are the same four sisters I grew up with during the first eighteen years of my life. Phyllis, Dorothy, Jeannie and Karen all crowded into my little condo. We partied for four days. We managed to eat, drink, walk for hours at a time, go to the theatre, shop and talk. The trips down memory lane were frequent and sometimes funny. We spent hours talking about our families and in particular our mothers. We laughed and we cried. Both of our mothers lost their lives to cancer but on this particular weekend we were focused on positive memories. In my heart I believe Phyllis and her sisters were here, not only to help celebrate my birthday, but to check on me physically as well. They needed to see for themselves that I was okay. March 28, 2009, we would also be celebrating my first year of being cancer free.

A breast cancer recurrence in 2008 altered the intended content of this book – a heavier slant on cancer than I had initially planned. Once again cancer frightened me and became front and centre in my world. I had big plans to celebrate my sixteen-plus years of being cancer free. It was not to be. This time I had to dig deeper than ever to stay out of depression's way. Cancer not only knocked on my door, it knocked me down physically and emotionally. Journalling the struggle of my recurrence from the beginning has been therapeutic and I am hopeful it will help others. Those who have been challenged by any life-threatening disease and those who simply see a bit of themselves in my story will relate to life's ups and downs.

At the request of many who have read *Lessons Learned Upside the Head* I have rewritten and added to the chapter offering advice about what to do when a loved one is facing cancer. You will see your input captured in the chapter called "Half-Past Cancer." Thanks so much to everyone who contacted me about this particular chapter.

The Comfort Heart Initiative continues to be my way of sharing my world with others and I am so grateful for the many connections this fundraiser has allowed me to make. In addition to raising money for cancer research this little pewter heart opens doors for many.

Mental illness wears many faces and is being talked about more openly than ever before. I am humbled by those who have shared their stories here. My own war with depression is not easy to speak about. If others can share, so can I.

I have learned to make and live with the hard decisions. A decision is never made easier simply because you know it is the right one. Moving away from my beloved Nova Scotia for the second time broke my heart and knowing I was doing it for all the right reasons didn't make it one bit easier. Regardless of my address, Nova Scotia will always be home for me and I have enjoyed writing about some who remain part of my life there.

My mother continues to influence my life so many years following her death from breast cancer. I am proud to include some of my favourite memories of Mary Rose Cole as well as stories about other women from my mother's era who have left their mark. I am forever interested in the topic of women in the workforce and I am disappointed that we don't see more women on national boards and in the corporate boardrooms. Have more women broken through the glass ceiling since I left the corporate world in 1994 as Vice President of Logistics after twenty-seven years with Bell Canada? Are women more supportive of each other today than when I was climbing the corporate ladder all those years ago? I ask these questions often. They are difficult to answer and often we don't like the answers.

I am a strong believer in journalling every day, another skill I learned from my mother. I am always interested in helping others as they begin to journal, and perhaps write their own memoir. Writing it down helps me solidify memories and it also helps me remove thoughts that I no longer want to carry around with me. Sometimes a negative thought leaves me completely when I put it on paper.

My Bell friends remain part of my life more than a decade after my retirement. We connect for very different reasons now than during the 1960s to 1990s period of my life. Priorities become clearer over time. So do friendships.

Through life's journey we face health issues and a body that doesn't always co-operate with what we think we should be able to do. We face reality as we make decisions about how we want our next twenty or forty years to play out. We battle our weight, and we battle our emotions. Our children come and go, and sometimes come and go again. Our grandchildren change our lives in the most delightful way. We face many issues and we strive to tackle everything thrown at us.

I have spoken with others who have graciously shared their inspirational life experiences. I have learned something from everyone I have spoken with and am grateful for their honesty and for sharing. In some cases you will read stories in their own words. Others have spoken with me at length and have allowed me to journal their story for you.

I hope you see a bit of yourself in *If I Knew Then What I Know Now* and, as always, I welcome your feedback.

"Don't Speak"

I somehow knew that cancer would hunt me down a second time. At least a second time. Hopefully not a third, but a second time without a doubt. I don't see this as being negative – just realistic. This would be one time I would hate being right.

I had recently moved back to Toronto and finding the right family physician was a high priority for me. I was relieved to learn that my doctor from my earlier days, Dr. David W. Tannenbaum, Family Physician-in-Chief at Mount Sinai Hospital, would take me as his patient once again. Dr. Tannenbaum suggested we order some tests to check my health completely. He would then have his own current test results for me and I would have the comfort of knowing I was back in the Mount Sinai system – a system that had looked after me so well all those years ago. A good feeling for a cancer survivor and a comforting memory to carry around.

We discussed whether or not the tests should include a mammogram. I had been having annual mammograms in Halifax and in fact in 2007 had had two. One in January showed something that needed to be checked again in six months. That second mammogram revealed nothing abnormal – certainly not cancer. Or so it was decided. At the time I made a mental note to pursue this at a later date. I found it negative to spend any energy in the moment wondering if something might have been missed in Halifax, so I decided to park my nagging doubts for the moment and tackle this when I had a confirmed clean bill of health. Live in the present. If something had been missed I would be wasting precious time looking back when I needed to look and move forward. Dr. Tannenbaum and I decided I would be booked for a mammogram even though only six months had passed since my last.

I have always loved the New Year and showed up for my January 3 mammogram filled with enthusiasm and hope. The New Year is always a fresh start. I shared with anyone who would listen that on January 27 I would be a sixteen-year cancer survivor. I did not want my record broken. No interruptions please.

A few days later the call came. Not totally unusual for me because I have been called back for a repeat mammogram before – several times over the decade. This time the call was for an enhanced mammogram scheduled for January 14. A cancer survivor will tell you that the wait between appointments is hell. I was thankful that my wait was not a long one, although every day felt like a lifetime.

On January 16 I was startled to receive another call. I would need a stereotactic biopsy of the breast and it had already been scheduled for January 24. Despite other callbacks over the years, this one frightened me. If it was "nothing" after a second mammogram in Halifax not much longer than six months ago, how can they be seeing something that requires a biopsy? I would soon find out. My emotional roller coaster ride began at warp speed and I felt helpless to slow it down.

In everyone's hectic schedule regardless of what is happening in your immediate world, life goes on. At this stage I had lots going on. I was able to set aside my cancer panic long enough to purchase a new condo in downtown Toronto. My real estate agent and friend, Eileen Savage, knew I wanted to live in an area I had coveted since the '70s. Eileen had been showing me real estate that I might be interested in for years and I felt no need to stop the process. I am one of those people who will go to an open house just to have a look. I tend to keep an eye on real estate news even when not actually looking to buy or sell – but this time I was looking. I had not yet sold my loft but was feeling like living on the edge so why not go for it? On Saturday, January 19, we found the perfect little spot for me. Found it – bought it – got that done.

On January 24 my son James came to town and we tried our best to keep busy leading up to my 1:30 p.m. biopsy appointment. We left my loft around 11 a.m. and checked out big screen TVs for my new condo. My current big screen measured about twelve inches so it could be argued that it was definitely time to replace it. This was one thing we could try to laugh about on a morning when we were digging very deep to find a sliver of humour. I could not make a decision. Nothing could take our minds off where we were headed, so we grabbed a fast lunch and made the dreaded walk to the hospital.

James has very little memory (selective in this case) of most of the details or his involvement during my first battle with breast cancer in January of 1992. He knows that both his mother and his grand-mother battled cancer at the same time and for a twenty-three-year-old that was enough to cope with – or not cope with. This time he was in it with me 100 percent – and we were about to be buried in it.

Some might tell you a stereotactic biopsy of the breast doesn't hurt much but let me describe my experience and you make your own decision. First your breast goes into the well-known squash-and-flatten-the-breast mammography machine. Then they freeze the breast area a little so the big hurt won't be a big hurt. Next a needle is inserted deep into the breast to get as close to the lump/mass/whatever as possible. Imagine that this needle has to be thick enough to allow a gun of sorts to shoot into that needle and grab and remove a sample of tissue. We (the survivors who have experienced this) call it a staple gun because even though we can't see it that is what it sounds like when the grab comes. The radiation technologists take considerable time getting you ready for the actual biopsy and thank God they do. They have to be very precise. To be fair, the pamphlet describing this procedure is much more positive. "Your breast will be moderately compressed using a special paddle that allows the radiologist to work through a small opening … The biopsy needle is passed through a small nick in the skin and 5 – 10 separate samples are taken through this one entry point." Sure.

The technologist tells you not to move and not to speak. Any little movement could alter what they have set up and even speak-ing could cause you to move – I guess. The first thing the radiologist does upon entering the room is say, "How are you doing, Miss Cole?" (He didn't read the "don't talk" manual.) The minute I speak both the technologist and the radiologist say in a not-too-low voice, "Please don't speak" and they go on to explain why. Silently my mind is telling them to stop speaking to me in the first place.

The radiologist, who is for the moment my new best friend, removes ten tissue samples and then he and the technologist leave the room to see what they have – to see if it is sufficient to make a diagnosis. Sadly, he comes back with the grim news that the samples are not good and they might have to use a small drill. I can't stay quiet. "Small drill is an oxymoron," I whisper while trying to not move even a fraction of an inch as I speak. "There is no such thing as a small drill when referring to the breast area." I am immediately told to stop talking. I do.

A second radiologist, who I assume might be the supervisor, enters the room, checks everything out both on their computer screen off in one corner and in the part of the room where they have me firmly stuck in the mammography machine with my head tilted up and back so it is out of the way. I can hear them but I can't see them because of the angle of my head at the moment. "Everything okay, Miss Cole?" Oh no you don't. I am not falling for that trick again so I don't reply. "I would like to try to remove some samples myself, Miss Cole. Can you stay like this for a while longer?" Sounds like she needs a reply, doesn't it? I begin to respond with, "I am doi ..." "DON'T SPEAK PLEASE."

Actually, I like this lady. She gives the air that she knows exactly what she is doing and after taking nine samples she leaves the room. Then she returns and announces that the torture is over. No drilling required. They will unhook me and send me home. She got the goods. As I approach my son in the waiting room the process appears to have been as hard on him as it was on me – almost. This is what I would describe as a bitch of a day. There would be more.

James gets me back home and comfortable before heading home to Tracey and Jalen in Barrie. It has been a very long day for him. I know he is worried. Me, not so much. I remain confident that I do not have cancer again. I can tell. I can feel in my body that I remain cancer free. I can feel it in my bones. Who am I kidding?

Later that same evening, because life goes on, Eileen put the wheels in motion to list my lovely little loft. I had enjoyed every second of it but it was never meant to be a permanent residence. I may have gotten a bit ahead of myself when I bought before selling the loft but that's me. As it turned out, the loft sold very fast, so that was one worry I did not have for more than a few days. Crossed it off my list.

I soon received a call from Dr. Wey Liang Leong's office. Dr. Leong is a surgical oncologist (one of the many hats he wears) and he would see me on February 19 to discuss pathology results. While the day loomed large I had conjured up my own reasons to believe this was not cancer. I continued to feel deep inside me that I remained cancer free and, more importantly, how could bad news come on the 19th? This was my sister Lois's sixty-fifth birthday. A time to celebrate. My horoscope on that day did concern me just a bit: "No matter how extrovert an Aries you may be the sun's transit of the most sensitive area of your chart will encourage you to give the party life a miss, at least for a while. What you think about over the next few weeks will form the basis of your life over the next twelve months, so think deeply and think well."

I made the decision to keep this appointment on my own. I was working hard to make it a normal day and if I brought James with me I felt that I would be conceding that I had a problem – a big problem. Dr. Leong was firm, compassionate and understanding and I liked him from the first second we met. A no-nonsense surgeon. And one who seemed very humane. He was quick to tell me the biopsy results were inconclusive and surgery would be required. He gently suggested that a mastectomy at this stage would likely mean no further surgery but I was having no part of it. No mastectomy. Not in my book. No way. I continued to be sure this was not cancer and I would run the risk of having surgery again two weeks later if I was wrong. It was my body – I knew I was not wrong. He understood my thinking and he accepted my decision. We parted with him telling me that his office would call me with a surgery date, hopefully within a few weeks. Less than two weeks if I was lucky. The wheels turned very quickly and surgery was booked.

My sister Connie arrived on February 26 to be with me for surgery the following day. Time had passed quickly and we were once again walking to Mount Sinai Hospital. We quietly walked past what had been my Bell home for years on the other side of University Avenue. So many memories on this street for me and on this side of the street the memories were not so positive. We could not help but reflect on that January day back in 1992 when we made a similar walk – Connie carried my stuff and I carried my cancer. Here we go again. Smarter minds would have taken a cab that particular February day. We were almost frozen solid when we arrived at 6:30 a.m. for out-patient surgery. Only two months into the new year and I wanted it to be over so I could begin the year again, ideally with a more positive outcome.

Before I could be taken to surgery a wire (yes, a wire) had to be inserted into my breast to guide the surgeon to where the mass could be located. The mammography machine was fast becoming a regular part of my life and I didn't like it. The happy technologist convinced me the needle that would allow the insertion of the wire was no more painful than the needle they would use to freeze the breast area so I really didn't need the freezing. I asked a few questions but in the end I was convinced. No freezing required. I am woman – I am strong.

The needle was inserted into my already battered breast and the technologist soon called someone in to view her good work – hit it on the first try. Again I had been instructed to remain silent and this time I knew enough to not contribute to the conversation. However, as they left me on my own and hovered over the computer screen I had to say, "Excuse me … I am fainting over here." One of them quickly pushed a pillow into my back to prevent me from falling (can't undo all of that good work getting the needle into the right spot on the first try) while the second threw some water on a cloth and then proceeded to throw it on my face. No fainting. No way. Honestly, it was funny – you had to be there.

I thought the procedure was finished, so you can imagine my surprise when the technologist said, "Now they have to insert the wire through the needle so stay very still." Like I could leave the room or move in any way. Surgery hadn't even happened yet and I felt done in.

I had only met Dr. Leong in an office setting and I liked him even better in the surgical setting. He came to talk with me pre-surgery; he personally walked me into the operating room and introduced me to everyone. He spoke with me a number of times post-surgery and also spoke with my sister directly after surgery. He gave us no reason to think we were out of the woods yet even though he felt the entire mass had been removed. We both liked his directness and his honesty, even if it hurt.

Two weeks later, on Thursday, March 13, Connie and I once again had an appointment at Mount Sinai. At 3:30 p.m. Dr. Leong would give us the pathology results. We were so sure I did not have cancer that we busied ourselves with many errands prior to getting to the hospital. We were expecting good news. We did a bit of shopping, I ordered new business cards and letterhead. We left home in the morning and yet were almost late arriving at the Mount Sinai breast clinic on the twelfth floor. To be honest, I find it a more pleasant place to be if you don't have cancer. Very few results-related hospital areas are pleasant if you have cancer. So many sad or anxious people hovering in the comfort of the clinic. My doctor was running late. I was Dr. Leong's last appointment for the day and I anxiously awaited his arrival in the little cubical I had been ushered into. "Place needs paint," I said aloud to no one as I looked around thinking of anything but the pathology results coming my way. I touched my breast wondering …

Dr. Leong entered the room and wasted no time. (Another thing I like about him.) Breast cancer. DCIS – ductal carcinoma in situ. Grade 2. I had to have further surgery – mastectomy.

I listened very carefully to my doctor's words and I thought back to January 1992 when I first entered the breast cancer arena. I am not the only breast cancer survivor to have a recurrence and so I would find a way to deal with it again. This time I would not be as fortunate – I would lose my breast. The one positive thing I could cling to came from my knowledge that DCIS of the breast is an early, localized cluster of cancer cells that start in the milk passage ducts of the breast but have not yet penetrated the duct walls into the surrounding tissue. The term "in situ" refers to a tumour that has not spread beyond the place where it originally developed.

More surgery to follow – soon we hoped. Connie and I left Mount Sinai with the terrible news. We cried for hours. And then we began making plans. I had a very long list – none of it pretty.

Making the first phone call to my son was the toughest call I have had to make.

Staging and a Passing Grade

"*If* I knew then what I know now" is a phrase that most of us have used at one time or another. Many cancer survivors use this expression when they experience a recurrence. We are fortunate to know so much more the second time around because it helps us answer our own questions and, more important, having knowledge helps us formulate the questions we need to ask.

When I had twenty-eight radiation treatments as part of my preventative package in 1992, it was explained to me that I would not be able to have radiation treatment again. At least, not in that specific breast area. When Grade 2 cancer came back in the same breast, I hoped I had remembered incorrectly, or that maybe – just maybe – things had changed and I could have radiation again. I knew the alternative would be a mastectomy. I feared this more than you can imagine.

For those who can have radiation there is some exciting news for breast cancer survivors. An alternative to traditional radiation therapy is being studied and used by Dr. Jean-Philippe Pignol, radiation oncologist at Sunnybrook's Odette Cancer Centre and Associate Professor in the Department of Radiation-Oncology at the University of Toronto. The procedure is called brachytherapy and can dramatically reduce side effects and prevent breast cancer recurrence. Instead of five weeks of radiation therapy, eligible women undergo a one-time procedure. Tiny rods of palladium are implanted, which emit radiation over a two-month period, allowing women to be treated while continuing their day-to-day activities. This is a great help, particularly for women living far from treatment centres who sometimes opt for mastectomy or refuse radiation treatment because of the difficulties of travel.

Dr. Pignol has said that a multi-year follow up study shows the procedure is highly effective in preventing breast cancer recurrence, and reduces the incidence of side effects five-fold. Quality of life questionnaires show that patients are satisfied. Dr. Pignol says, "The most striking comment was, 'I didn't feel I was a cancer patient.' The Canadian Breast Cancer Foundation is absolutely unique in promoting this sort of research." I have met Dr. Pignol personally. He is very committed to the work he does and is a wonderful friend to breast cancer survivors.

While writing this chapter I contacted Dr. Pignol to make sure he was supportive of me quoting him. I also asked if there was any other news he could share that would be positive for women to hear at this time. He replied that as of November 2008, "We have treated sixty-seven patients, real Canadian heroes, from 2004 to 2007 and as we are reaching the five years follow-up landmark we do not have any patient with recurrence. The seed implant technique has five times less acute side effects compared to standard treatment and patients are very satisfied with the procedure. Since January 2008 I am working on two trials:

"1. A Registry trial to capture possible rare side effects of the technique. This trial will be open in several centres in the States and in Canada and hence allow more women to access the procedure. This trial has been made possible through a generous multimillions donation from the Odette family.

"2. A Phase II trial for DCIS, Ductal Carcinoma in Situ. This trial will test to see if the technique could be offered to pre-invasive cancer patients that nowadays represent 22 percent of breast cancer patients. The study will be run simultaneously in Ottawa and Toronto and is funded through a very generous grant from the Canadian Breast Cancer Foundation."

Unfortunately, no brachytherapy for me. Dr. Leong explained, and my sister Lorraine confirmed, that indeed I could not have radiation in the same area a second time. I had been given the total allowable dosage in 1992 and if radiated again the cells would not heal – in fact, the skin tissue would break down and never heal.

The word "staging" was used with my first cancer but not the word "grade" so I had another learning curve ahead of me this time. My recurrence was Grade 2. I soon learned and understood the difference between the two.

The stage of the tumour tells us where the tumour is and the size, the node involvement and whether or not the cancer has spread to other organs (metastases). There are four stages. Stage 0 indicates that the cancerous tumour has not broken out of the ducts – it is not invasive. Stage 1 indicates some evidence of breaking out of the ducts, there are no nodes involved and the cancerous tumour measures two centimetres or less. At Stage 2 the tumour measures two to five centimetres and has exhibited some evidence of breaking out of the ducts. It may have already spread to the lymph nodes. Stages 3 and 4 show increasing tumour size, nodal involvement and spread to other organs.

The grade of a tumour refers to the growth pattern and what the tumour is. Grade 1 indicates a slow-growing tumour, Grade 2 a moderate growth pattern and Grade 3 fast-growing tumours. Grade is all about how the cancer cells are acting and what they look like.

So much information – and so many important decisions to be made.

Birthday Preparations

*S*oon after my March 13 appointment I received the call confirming my next surgery date. On March 28 I would have a mastectomy and sentinel lymph node biopsy. Happy birthday to me. I am not sure any day in my life could rival this day for the sadness and depression that came with this call. I knew it was coming but that didn't make it any easier to hear.

There was much to be done and it was not all related to my surgery. The sale of my loft was about to close. I still had things to move out, and other things to purchase and move to my new condo. Additionally, I wanted to find a breast prosthetic place that was right for me. Literature suggests most women are ready for their fitting four to six weeks after surgery and while I was not looking for a fitting at this stage, I was looking for the place where all this would happen. I needed to meet the right person and be able to visualize the business location where I would be both comfortable and looked after. And I needed it now. I did not care that the literature said "now" was too soon.

My first priority, though, was my family. On Easter Sunday Jalen came to town with his mom and dad and we took a break from cancer to enjoy Easter together. Viewing my new condo for the first time was totally lost on Jalen as the Easter egg hunt took place. He found all of the eggs in record time and months later was still asking, "Nana, where are the eggs?" Actually, when I think back, a month following Christmas he was trying to secretly hang his stocking so Santa could visit one more time – perhaps there is a trend here. Smart kid. Spending the day with my son, with Tracey and this wonderful little boy brought a sense of reality to my world and I was able to forget about cancer for a few hours. I had so much to live for. This time with family was wonderful therapy for me.

A day or two later as I reflected once again on my need to find exactly where I would purchase my prosthesis, I thought back to November 2006 when I had spoken at a conference hosted by Amoena Canada Inc. Amoena makes breast prosthetics as well as specialty bras and other garments. The conference was for Amoena clients – businesses that sold Amoena products. The conference had been a magical evening and didn't feel like work at all. In fact, it was anything but work. It was close to my heart and to the hearts of everyone in attendance. The evening was about celebrating women: clients, customers and the memory of all those we have lost. While the mood was happy and light, there were tears and lots of raw emotion. Amoena's business is, quite frankly, all about raw emotion. As a bit of an outsider in terms of the competitive edge that must exist between many of the Amoena clients present that evening, I was profoundly touched to watch them come together so easily in their common goal – to help women after breast surgery.

There were many women at the conference who, for different reasons, I bonded with and have kept in touch with. Of course, at the time I didn't consider for one minute that I would be in touch with some of them for very personal reasons at a later date. Carol Bond and I joined some of the women at the bar later that evening and, in particular, I remember speaking with Lori Vanhapelto, who owns Brand New You in Thunder Bay, Ontario. Our conversation moved quickly from breast cancer to mothers. Lori confided that her mother suffered from Alzheimer's and was living in a nursing home. Rather than have the home do her mom's laundry Lori chose to do it for her – it gave her the feeling that she could always ensure her mom would look nice and additionally it felt good to be doing personal things for her mother. We talked at length about the bond between mothers and their daughters.

I had been booked to speak at the conference by Voula Pantelis, General Manager of Amoena, and we had kept in touch following the conference. Now I found myself calling Voula, sharing my recurrence details and asking her to refer me to someone in my area I could work with, relate to and be comfortable with. Voula introduced me to Melanie Heenan, owner of Melmira Bra and Swimsuits on Yonge Street. The front of the Melmira brochure says, "Where women restore a positive body image, confidence and self-esteem." For me, it was important that I make this contact prior to my surgery so four days pre-surgery I met Melanie. It was on my list of things to do. Type A personality. I needed to see what was out there, what might work for me and how I would feel walking into her store. It all worked. Melanie is a seasoned business woman with considerable experience and a heart that truly understands and relates to her clients. I liked her immediately. Before I left, Melanie gave me gifts from Amoena, including a post-surgical camisole that I would soon learn was worth its weight in gold. We talked about my return visit, which would be some four to six weeks post-surgery when I would be fitted for my breast prosthesis. I could hardly say the words. Melanie promised to work with me personally. I was very grateful.

Melanie had also been in the audience that evening when I spoke at the Amoena conference. In fact, we sat at the same table prior to my introduction. Her daughters work with her in her business and they had been there as well. I was happy to have met her on a previous occasion. It seemed to help me control my emotions just a little bit.

Three days prior to surgery Connie and I attended a "Survivorship class" at the hospital. We heard from a nurse who explained the mastectomy procedure and the care that would be required to ensure that the incision healed as it should and that the drainage tube was managed properly. The room was full of cancer patients and each of us brought a family member with us. It seemed that everyone had to fight to have their family member attend because of space restrictions. We all felt that it was essential we have someone with us, and it seemed both negative and unnecessary to watch and listen to the exchange repeated over and over again as either the survivor or the family member insisted that the survivor needed someone with her. I personally missed much of what was being said because I was so nervous. Thank God Connie was there – taking notes. I meant to follow up and offer feedback on this particular rule. I felt badly for the clerical staff trying to enforce this "no one but the patient" rule. It was not easy for them. Everything else was positive and if this could be addressed the day would run much more smoothly for everyone involved. I do understand space restrictions but this has to change and it's on my list of things to address. Everyone needs an advocate at a time like this. As self-confident and aggressive as I can be, I needed Connie to help me get through this particular day. I knew I was not "myself."

A dietician spoke with us and we also heard from a social worker. As I listened to Trisha, the social worker, speak about our emotional recovery I knew I would ask for help. During my first battle with breast cancer my Comfort Heart Initiative seemed to serve as my therapist but this time I would need more. Trish spoke of fear, anxiety, sadness, a sense of loss, grieving, crying, anger and frustration. She made so much sense. Connie and I left the hospital feeling pretty numb. I called Trish later to tell her how much I appreciated all that she shared with us that day. She helped me make my initial call requesting therapy.

Both Connie and I required some retail therapy the following day, so we went on the hunt for a lamp and bought a coffee table instead. That evening my son and his buddy Brent came to town and installed not one but two big screen TVs for me. We were forty-eight hours away from surgery. If nothing else, my home was ready.

The following day, on March 27, James came back to Toronto and bunked in with Connie and me. We had big plans for the following morning – my birthday.

The Mother of all Birthdays – March 28, 2008

*T*here would be no mention of having a happy birthday on this particular morning. We had agreed to have a belated birthday celebration when this was all behind us. Connie, James and I awoke early to make the trek again to Mount Sinai Hospital.

There is something soothing for me in walking to the hospital, giving me time to mentally prepare and clear my head of any and all negative energy. This particular morning there was little of anything but fright on my mind. Everyone who passed by was no one in particular and yet I looked at each person wondering what their day might look like. Hopefully, they were rushing to the work room not to the operating room. Between my sister, my son and me few words were spoken and yet we knew we were speaking the same language.

We were scheduled to arrive several hours prior to surgery because I would be having a procedure that was barely on the radar sixteen years ago when I first presented with breast cancer. Lymph node removal has come a long way from January of 1992 when I had thirteen lymph nodes removed in a procedure that would require a very long recovery time. You will hear breast cancer survivors speak about how terrible and how lengthy the recovery from lymph node removal can be. The pain and the recovery time is often far worse and much longer than the pain from the breast surgery incision itself. With the advances being made in surgery, all of this has been replaced in many cases with the sentinel lymph node (SLN) biopsy. I took the time to research and understand the procedure prior to surgery day.

When breast cancer cells begin to spread from the main tumour site in the breast, they travel to the lymph nodes in the underarm area. The first lymph node they reach is the sentinel lymph node. An SLN biopsy is a diagnostic procedure used to determine if the breast cancer has spread (metastasized) to any of the auxiliary lymph nodes. The actual procedure requires the removal of only one or two lymph nodes for the pathologist to review. If the sentinel nodes do not contain cancer cells, this could eliminate the need to remove additional lymph nodes in the auxiliary area.

Having read that the SLN biopsy can result in less pain and fewer complications, I was hoping this would be the case for me. In particular, I remember not only how painful it was but also how long it took to regain my normal range of motion with my left arm following my 1992 surgery. I was praying science has truly seen advances in this area.

My son came with me for the actual SLN biopsy. I needed James by my side for as long as possible on this day. I didn't know the details regarding how the procedure would evolve and had not realized that a needle would actually be inserted into my nipple area to begin the procedure. James got to leave the room for that part.

I was beginning to realize why I had to arrive so early – this procedure would take more than a few minutes. For starters, a small dose of a low-level radioactive tracer called technetium-99 was inserted into the breast. Technetium-99 contains less radiation than a standard x-ray and they tell me it is relatively safe. I should have realized a needle in the nipple would hurt. At the same time, a blue dye is injected to help visually track the location of the sentinel node during the surgery.

I was warned that for any number of reasons, this might not work in my case. Initially it looked like it would not. No nodes appeared on the computer screen. I could not actually see the screen but my son could and he kept me informed moment by moment. At one point, it was decided that we would stop the procedure, and I was instructed to massage the nipple area to see if this would stimulate movement of the dye to the SLN. It was not lost on me that this would probably be the last time I would touch my breast – by day's end it would be gone. A number of technologists were in and out of the room and finally, after what seemed like hours but was likely not more than thirty minutes, a node was found.

Eureka – we can move on to surgery. During the procedure my surgeon, Dr. Leong, arrived to check on things. And, I think, to remind everyone that we were running behind and an operating room with a full medical team was awaiting my arrival. Things moved very quickly after Dr. Leong entered the room but not so much that the personal touch was lost. He took time to meet my son and shake his hand. That meant a lot to me.

Given how I was positioned in the SLN room I really could not see the room itself or the people moving in and out. I asked James to journal the visuals and also his emotions at that time. Here is what he wrote:

We were in the waiting room, actually in the hallway next to the waiting room, my mom in a wheelchair in surgical clothing. She looked so small, tired and worst of all scared. This was the hard part for me as I could not fix it. It was what it was.

The gentleman who was going to do the procedure came and asked Mom questions. Then he promptly left. Back to the waiting. Another woman came and got us. We were informed that only my aunt Connie or I could accompany Mom for her test. I suggested that my aunt go. I was thinking that my mother would be better served with another female point of view. My mom wanted me.

I had a few moments alone with the technician before the procedure. She had all the personality that the gentleman before didn't. I admit I understand the guy: this job sucks and how do you have small talk with people before they lose a breast? However, she was different. She had a great smile and an attitude that rivalled Snoopy when he danced. I wish I could remember her name. She was great. Sadly, she was just covering the other guy's break.

Each test would take five minutes (in fact the screen would count from 300 seconds). During the first test it was explained that we were looking for a glowing dot to show up on the screen. The first 300 seconds counted down slowly. No dot.

During the second test Mom explained to me that if no dot showed up it could mean there were no lymph nodes to be found at this stage. If this was the case we would not be able to find out if the cancer had spread using this procedure. It made the surgery almost feel secondary. No dot.

The seconds seemed to slow down. Third test turned out the same. My mother was more upset than I had ever seen her. I was heartbroken. This may have been the saddest point of my life. We talked about how there clearly were no lymph nodes.

Fourth test … no dot.

We took a break. Mom would have to massage her breast to get the dye to hopefully move. The technician repositioned the machine, started it and left the room. This was it – last test. I stood on the other side of the machine so I could talk to Mom. She could not see the screen as I could. We had succumbed to the thinking that it was over. Then the best part of my day. In came the female technician to get something from the room. A shy smile as I'm sure she knew what had been happening since she left. While at the desk she looked to the screen and very confidently pointed and said, 'There's one!' And she changed the resolution on the screen to show it to me. I teared up and told Mom that we have to make a deal to never make a diagnosis on our own ever again.

On a day like this, with so much negativity, it felt like a win. I agree a small win.

Next stop – the operating room. I had been here before, only two weeks earlier. Some of the faces were the same. I was in good hands and sleeping before I could realize things had happened already. The surgery was scheduled to be approximately two hours and ran a bit longer than that.

When I awoke in the Recovery Room I immediately felt to see if my breast was still there. I knew it would be gone but I had to check. My heart sank for myself and for all of the women before (and sadly, after) me who had shared this experience. Life is so not fair. How would I get my life back on track? Happy freaking birthday to me.

There was not a lot of time to think about getting my life back on track, or about anything else in fact. I would be in the hospital for twenty-four hours only. I didn't sleep much that night, not so much because of pain but because of the emotional turmoil I seemed to be swimming in. How would I move forward this time? I was sixteen years older for starters and didn't have my "big job at the Bell" to occupy much of my mental time.

Me, Lois, Lorraine and Connie.

It seems a small thing now, but one thing upset me to no end during that short hospital stay and it could have so easily been avoided. The day nurse, as she was leaving at her shift's end, advised me that my IV could be removed but that she needed to leave that for the night nurse to deal with. She was incredibly busy and I got that. The night nurse advised me it was not her responsibility and that my IV would in fact stay with me until the day nurse returned in the morning. I kept thinking, "My God, I can't even manage the simple removal of an IV." I got over that as my IV pole and I paced the hospital corridors during a sleepless night. In the morning I spoke with the day nurse about how this had made me feel. She felt badly and all was forgiven. As I said, she was incredibly busy.

As I walked the halls during the night I thought about my sisters. Surely to God they would never have to experience this first-hand – it was bad enough they had to go through it with me yet again. Whenever I meet sisters who have both battled breast cancer my thoughts automatically go to my own. As I paced I carried with me a positive image of the four of us together a few years ago as we celebrated Connie's fiftieth. Photographer and friend Sue Mills had taken many photos and she captured us so well. I especially love the informal shots. I hung on to an image of us relaxing and laughing "between takes" until morning came and I had more pressing issues to deal with.

Within twenty-four hours I was being released from the hospital. I soon learned how valuable my new post-surgical camisole would be. I had lost a breast but gained a drainage tube with a tidy little sack at the end of the tube. This small sack could be tucked away in the almost invisible pouch on the inside of my camisole. Who knew? Home care would visit me each day until my drainage tube and I were separated.

I thanked everyone at Mount Sinai, including my day nurse, and in a flash my friend Eileen helped Connie pack me into her car and home I went. My birthday had come and gone and now so had I.

As Eileen helped Connie move me from car to condo she also gave me a wonderful gift – a Braun Tassimo coffee machine. Now I could make my own lattes – while still in my pajamas. During my recovery time this would be an especially great gift for me. That all-important first cup of coffee each morning is always a gift. On this day I was reminded to be thankful for small things.

This was a birthday I won't forget anytime soon.

Pathology Results and the Invitation

Pathology results loomed large as Connie and I rose just after 6 a.m. to greet the day. We enjoyed more than one latte and the quiet of the early morning as we began to talk about the day. The papers were read and discarded, the housework was done, we were dressed and ready to go – it was now 7:30 a.m. My appointment time with Dr. Leong was many hours away. Colour us anxious.

We had already made the decision that if pathology results were good (meaning no more cancer) Connie would return home to Nova Scotia the following day. We spent a bit of time packing her things and talking about when I would be going home to visit and her possible next visit to Toronto. So far, this year was shaping up like no other in terms of us being unable to carry out plans. We always have plans.

James and Tracey had already made the decision that results would definitely bring good news. They are always so positive. The wheels were in motion for a belated birthday party to take place that same night at Nana's. Jalen was so excited. A party in the mind of a three-year-old means balloons, an invitation and cake. There is nothing more delightful than seeing a party through the eyes of a three-year-old.

Connie and I decided to make an adventure out of the morning. We walked for miles and followed that with a shopping opportunity when we realized we were heading in the direction of the Eaton Centre. I was positive but still not focused. Connie had better luck shopping and found a nice pair of summer capri pants. After all, summer was not far away.

While waiting for Connie outside of a store in the Eaton Centre I ran into a friend of mine from my Bell days. I was feeling very vulnerable at the time and this was a friend I had lost touch with, so seeing him so unexpectedly in the middle of the day said something to me. We first met in the mid '70s on the job at Bell in Kingston, Ontario, and we had considerable history.

Why do friends lose touch? Why do we let that happen? I didn't have any answers that day and I still don't. Sadly, some friendships don't survive and on that particular day I couldn't shake the sadness of this man and I having lost touch. I felt badly after I blurted out, "I am on my way to find out if I have breast cancer." He gave me a hug, asked for my business card and said he would be in touch to see if I was okay. We went our separate ways. He didn't follow up. I didn't either. I should have been the bigger person and called. My excuse was that I had other things on my mind – just an excuse. I like to think we really are still friends – just guilty of not taking the time to connect.

Finally we could delay it no longer – we checked in at Mount Sinai Hospital and I waited for my turn to see the good doctor. Connie had to wait outside and was left to see family member after family member being called in to be with various patients who had seemingly been given bad news. It made for many delays and a very long afternoon. I waited for over an hour and filled my time doing my arm exercises, praying that I would be strong and healthy again soon. I checked my incision one more time. Is there any cancer left there? I would wonder silently again and again. At one point I left my cubicle to tell Connie I had not seen the doctor yet so in this case no news did not mean good news. It didn't mean anything at all.

When Dr. Leong was finally able to get to me he spared no time in giving me the good news – Grade 2 mass – got it all – nodes, both of them, were clear – I heard the words I was hoping for. "You are cancer free. Go live your life." Thank you, Jesus! (I said that, not Dr. Leong.)

In reality, it didn't actually happen that fast. Dr. Leong apologized for being late. I totally understood. I would have waited until midnight for this good news. He suggested that other than coming to see him in six months I needed no further follow-up at this time.

Me, Barb, Faith and Connie.

My mind told me I needed a couple of things. I wanted to be referred to medical oncology. In particular I wanted to see Dr. Martin Blackstein, who had held my hand all those years ago when cancer was so new to me. I needed his opinion. His opinions – on everything – matter to me. For example, on May 28, 1992, Dr. Blackstein noted in my file, "I have reinforced some warnings about tanning and sun protection for this summer. She is obviously quite a sunbather." We had had a discussion that particular day about my suntan. It was only a few months post-surgery plus radiation yet I was clearly spending too much time in the sun. When I read his note in my file years later, I was reminded of how much time Dr. Blackstein had spent with me helping me with so many issues. I did learn the don't sunbathe lesson finally.

Secondly, I knew I was not healing all that well emotionally. In fact, I was an emotional train wreck in my unprofessional opinion so I asked Dr. Leong to refer me to a therapist. He set the wheels in motion that very day for both of those things to happen.

Connie and I went home to call or e-mail a million people (thirty for sure) with the good news. Next we eagerly awaited the beginning of the birthday celebration.

We met Jalen and his parents in the lobby where I was holding a guest parking pass for their car. Jalen saw the piece of paper in my hand and began shouting, "Nana, what is that paper? Is that your invitation? Did you get an invitation to the party too?" He jumped into my arms and announced, "Nana, I have a very very very very (four very's) big present for you." Let the party begin.

Life is good. I was happy to be sixty-two – and thankful to be alive to celebrate it.

There would be many birthday celebrations for me in 2008. Some were before my actual birthday and before I knew my cancer was back. Faith Deloughery and her partner Bill invited us to their home for an early March party. Bill snapped this photo (on page 35) of me preparing to have birthday cake with Barb, Faith and Connie. A second biopsy had just taken place and a few days after this photo was taken I would hear the pathology results – cancer. Again. Even though I believe you can see a slight hesitation in my smile, this was a joyful and thankful day for me surrounded by family and friends who would be by my side no matter what lay ahead.

Cancer is tougher on those who are dead.

The Fitting

*T*hree weeks post-surgery I decided it was time for the fitting – the dreaded fitting that would make the entire experience even more real. For sixteen years I had escaped this but now could put it off no longer.

The Toronto sky was clear except for a bit of fog as I opened my eyes and enjoyed my east-facing view. Maybe if we didn't have so much fog I could see east all the way to home. The weather report said it would be 20 degrees later, a good day to be outside. I made the call and the appointment for that same day.

I did what I do so well when there is something on my to-do list that I am dreading. I dance around it. I went to the post office. I checked out a printing place where I could have a book proposal copied closer to my new home. I picked up a few groceries (marshmallows for Jalen because he remained hopeful that we could light a fire and roast marshmallows on my little balcony on the twenty-first floor). I shopped for a new top to wear when I went home to Nova Scotia in a couple of weeks (maybe) and then I sat and replied to every single e-mail in my in-basket. I did all of this knowing there would be one thing left on my list – the fitting. It wouldn't go away.

Eventually I would take the subway to reach my destination but first I needed to walk and bask in the warm weather. And walk. And walk. My plan was to visit a few shops north of where I live. I poked in a few, bought a birthday gift for my friend Clare and a few things for my gift stash in another, but as I exited the quaint little shop I realized I hadn't really seen half of what I had looked at. My mind was all over the map yet again. I had no further interest in shopping. I wanted only to get this over with. Not the most positive attitude, I realize, but I am being honest.

I tried very hard and finally was able to totally focus on my mission – with one exception. I saw walking towards me a man I had once gone out with. I can't ever really say we dated because our few times together were sporadic and strange to say the least. I will call him Bob. He was dressed in his casual business attire with his trademark long blond hair (I love the look of long hair on a man) and cigarette dangling (not such a good look on anyone). He wore a crisp white dress shirt with the top few buttons undone. I'm not sure I had ever seen him in anything else. His chosen uniform looked good on him as always. I made an instant decision that I did not feel well enough to stop and do that dance that says, "My God, how are you? It's been so long. You haven't changed a bit. We must catch up. I will call you." Seems he made the same decision because we passed each other with only the slightest glance. He didn't even break his conversation with the man walking with him. I could learn from him. He ignores better than I do. Note to self – work on that skill in case you see him again.

I arrived at my destination early of course; I am early for everything. I found a little coffee shop where I could escape with my thoughts until my appointed time. I thought of all the women I know who have been in my shoes and how they have dealt with this and moved on. Why was it all such an emotional issue for me? I purchased a bottle of water and a morning glory. A muffin morning glory, not the liquid kind, albeit I could have used the fortification of the liquid refreshment. I checked for any new e-mails, read a bit and people-watched. I watched a very elderly lady pushing her cart through the intersection. The light had long turned red as she maneuvred her cart companion forward. The smile on her face suggested that all was well with her world. The temperature had reached 20 degrees and she was dressed for the summer sunshine in a long-sleeved sundress in a bright, bold print and a wide-brimmed hat that covered all but her radiant smile. If she was a breast cancer survivor you certainly could not tell by looking at her. Lesson learned.

My mind wandered and I could not focus on the present. For sixteen years I had been cancer free. When I had a lumpectomy, they called it a simple lumpectomy. At the time I suggested that had been yet another oxymoron – no such thing as a simple lumpectomy. Now I realized how simple that earlier surgery had been. I didn't even have an indentation where the scar had been and often when I went for my yearly mammogram I would have to point out to the technologist where the incision had been. The scar was completely gone and my breast revealed no signs of what once was. No signs on the outside anyway.

Back to the present – showtime. I walked slowly, with my head down and my heart pounding, to the Melmira Bra & Swimsuits door. For a second I thought, "I can't open the door – too heavy. Maybe this is a sign – go home and come back another time." I had been having trouble opening doors since my special birthday experience and this was no exception. I tried a bit harder – the door opened.

Clearly, this is not a store for breast cancer survivors only. I immediately liked that. When I am at the hospital, during breast cancer Thursday clinic for example, I am surrounded by survivors and that can be both good and bad. That's another story. At Melmira I saw women both young and old leave the store with their purchase, their chin in the air and their confidence intact. Maybe it wouldn't be so bad after all. Melanie greeted me immediately. We had met some years ago when I spoke at the Amoena conference and again more recently when I consulted with her a few days prior to surgery to get a very general understanding of what was in store for me – or in her store for me in this case. With some trepidation I revealed my scar to Melanie – a scar from centre chest to deep in the underarm. Healing well but an ugly scar none the less in my opinion. A scar where a breast is supposed to be. A scar where a breast once was. I cried. Melanie stood quietly beside me – exactly what I needed her to do.

Melanie took the time to fit me for the proper breast prosthesis and to help me to choose new bras that would be modified to hold my breast form. I spent a very long time looking at bras before making my selection. I wondered if I would ever enjoy shopping for a bra again. For now I had made my selection and would return a few days later to pick up my modified bras. I felt confident that returning would not be as difficult as today had been. I had taken a very large step towards recovery but I still had miles to go.

I walked for over two hours on the way home. I cried. I tried to visualize myself being positive about wearing a prosthesis as I live my daily life. I tried telling myself to get over it. There are people far worse off – didn't work. I was knee-deep in a pity party and that was where I needed to be.

I vowed to get over it – later.

Fifth World Conference on Breast Cancer

From June 4 to June 8, 2008, over six hundred people gathered at the Winnipeg Convention Centre for the Fifth World Conference on Breast Cancer. The theme struck a chord with me – Heart, Soul and Science: It's a Small World After All. I'll say.

It was a bit soon after my recurrence to spend time with so many breast cancer survivors, but I had made a commitment to Barb Shumeley long before my diagnosis. Barb is a good friend and was President of the Fifth World Conference. Initially, I wanted to be there for her. In the end, I was there for me and it was a four-day therapy session.

At certain times during the conference it seemed to be too much – even the *Winnipeg Free Press* was pink on the opening day. Not everyone approved of that but my hat was off to the paper for being willing to make such a bold statement of support. I found myself reading the paper front to back each day. I wanted to get inside the head of a paper that had made a difference to so many survivors on one particular day in their lives.

While the World Conference Board of Directors ensured that equal status was given to survivors, it was clear that we shared the stage with some extremely important people. We met and listened to renowned experts on all facets of breast cancer including prevention, diagnosis, treatment, research, the holistic approach, social services and so many challenges faced by survivors and their families.

I met people from India, Egypt, Philippines, Norway, Australia, New Zealand, China, Spain, Ireland, France, England, Nigeria, Canada and the USA. I collected so many business cards and e-mail addresses I spent most of my time en route back to Toronto when the conference ended going through the cards and making personal notes to help me remember everyone.

Dr. Annie Sasco and I met during a cab ride from the Winnipeg airport to our hotel. She arrived from France with carry-on luggage only and even before knowing who she was, I was immediately impressed. I am a great believer in never checking luggage. There was more to come. Dr. Sasco is the team leader of epidemiology for Cancer Prevention at the INSERM research unit at the medical school of the Université Victor Segalen Bordeux 2 in France. (INSERM is the only French public institute entirely dedicated to biological, medical research and improving public health.) After she completed medical school, Dr. Sasco attended Harvard University in the USA where she earned, not one, but two Master's degrees and a doctorate in epidemiology.

A Nobel Peace Prize nominee in 2005, Dr. Sasco is a very strong advocate for women in the sciences. Her major goal is to contribute to the inspiration and formation of future generations of scientists and citizens, starting at home with her own children. This woman speaks French, English and Italian, and when she spoke at the conference her words hit home with every survivor. She spoke a language we could all relate to. Once she took the stage, she did not leave it willingly.

Dr. Sasco's talk was titled "The Greatest Threat to Women's Health: Breast Cancer in the World" and she began by saying, "I have not had breast cancer – yet." She dedicated her presentation to those killed by breast cancer, those already sick and fighting hard and the ones who do not yet have this terrible disease. Early in her presentation she said something that was very personal to me. She was instrumental in getting tamoxifen classified as a carcinogen and therefore not best for prevention. I had taken tamoxifen for five long years and this gave me lots to think about.

Her presentation spoke about genetics and familial risk factors, the BRACA1 and BRACA2 genes among others. Dr. Sasco made us think about our nutrition, exercise, the environment, alcohol consumption and smoking. I have heard many others speak on all of these topics but the passion was greater this day. In particular, I could relate to one of her slides. It read, "Prevention of millions of cancer cases and deaths in the world in the twenty-five years to come is feasible based on the knowledge we have today. It is a matter of political will and therefore of citizens' action. As a woman, epidemiologist, and citizen of the world, I am just trying to contribute to that goal."

Of all the people I had the pleasure of speaking with, one of the most meaningful was Barb Shumeley's mother. I have such a soft spot in my heart for mothers and for a very brief moment I met Hilda Collett. Mrs. Collett attended the gala celebration as the World Conference came to an end, just a few weeks before her ninety-fifth birthday. Having battled breast cancer many years ago she is a symbol of hope to all breast cancer survivors. Mrs. Collett is a beautiful woman inside and out.

I had the honour – and it was truly an honour – of addressing the conference with a talk that I called "When Cancer Brings Clarity." I shared many of those things in my life that have become even more clear with my recurrence – family, friends and not living a materialistic life. In other words, not so much clutter around me both physically and emotionally. At the end of my talk I experienced such an emotional moment and one that was a gift I will cherish forever.

Trying to bring a bit of humour to my talk I explained that my recurrence, my mastectomy surgery, took place on my birthday and that while I had told many people in the hospital it was my birthday no one sang "Happy Birthday" to me. When I finished my presentation, I moved to centre stage to bow and receive the warm applause from the audience. As I stood there, over six hundred people stood up and sang "Happy Birthday." You can't imagine how wonderful I felt at that very moment. Of course, I cried. I later learned it was my soon-to-be-best-friends from Cape Breton who energized the crowd from their table at the back of the room and with their magic way of bringing people together, they began the song.

Women, for the most part, wear makeup and during one of the presentations we learned that toxins, carcinogens and ingredients that act like estrogen, which helps breast cancer tumours grow, are found in all kinds of makeup, perfume, hair-care, grooming and beauty products. Many of the ingredients discussed are foreign to us; phthalates, propyl and methyl parabens, butyl hydroxy anisole (BHA) formaldehyde and alpha-hydroxy acids are a few common ingredients that pose potential health risks. One website we can use to educate ourselves is www.cosemeticsdatabase.com. You hear these things as you rush to read the paper in your busy day but sitting at this conference and taking the time to drink in the words made us all think.

In 2006 the Canadian government required that all cosmetics sold had to list their ingredients on the packaging but, the catch is, if we don't know which ingredients are harmful we can't possibly make informed choices. I learned that the manufactures of cosmetics are not required to demonstrate safety and in a world where we try to make ourselves look good to feel better I came away from the conference questioning some of the makeup that I purchase. It's a start.

Breast cancer's effects on sex and image were also discussed at the conference. Anne Katz, a sexuality counsellor at Cancer Care Manitoba, reminded us that our brain is the biggest sex organ. I spoke with some very young breast cancer survivors who discuss the sexual issue right up front and leave nothing unspoken. "Everything on the table" is their motto.

Lisa Tugnette, author of *Reflections of a Woman – my memoir of breast cancer: loss, love & laughter*, and I had spoken via e-mail prior to June 4 and were able to meet and spend a bit of time together at the conference. Lisa is a beautiful woman. She was diagnosed with breast cancer at the age of thirty-six and shares so much of herself in her memoir. For me, the revealing photos of her before and after her breast reconstruction offered a powerful education. She gives generously through these photos and I suspect many survivors trying to make that all-important decision about breast reconstruction will be stronger in their resolve to make their decision, to have or not to have reconstruction, after reading Lisa's book and studying the photos she shares.

There are many things in addition to being breast cancer survivors that Lisa and I have in common – we shared the breast cancer stage with our mothers and we have both been blessed to call our mothers our friends as well. We recall the sad looks on our mothers' faces as we left home at the tender age of eighteen and we have memories of alcoholic fathers. I am proud to mentor Lisa in some small way.

I elected to attend one workshop that would introduce me to Dr. Ritu Biyani-Joseph, who spoke about the "Milestones of Highways Beyond Cancer." The title of her presentation intrigued me and as I listened to her tell her story I felt such admiration for her. Dr. Biyani-Joseph drove solo some 30,220 kilometres in 177 days to the four tips of India. She drove across the world's highest motorable mountain passes, Khardung La, 18,630 feet above sea level in Ladakh, India, and many other major high-altitude passes. Her presentation came to life as she showed slides of many individuals she had met and the vast lands she travelled. Dr. Biyani-Joseph conducted 140 awareness programs reaching out to more than 26,000 people in remote regions. With her through much of this journey was her daughter, Tista, who we also met during her presentation. The bond and the connection between mother and daughter were very evident and touching. You can learn more about her at her website (www.highwaysbeyondcancer.org).

Throughout the conference I was reminded that breast cancer knows no age boundaries. I met a thirty-year-old breast cancer survivor, Lindsay MacPhee from Cape Breton. She was diagnosed at twenty-seven. Lindsay and I share a cancer experience, a love of Louis Vuitton, stilettos, a history that includes big jobs and closeness with our mothers. It breaks my heart that women as young as Lindsay are forced to face this killer disease and, on a bad day, I worry that we will never find the damn cure. But then I remember Lindsay's motto and my spirits are lifted. She boldly says, "I am kickin' cancer in the ass with my stilettos."

One of the positive elements of these conferences is that they offer a network for women. Netta More from Mahalakshmi Mumbai and I found a way to speak the same language. She asked me to send her a copy of *Lessons Learned Upside the Head* and that was the first thing on my to-do-list when I returned to Toronto. After reading my book she sent me a wonderful e-mail and I know we will stay in touch. So many women reaching out to each other as a result of this conference give me hope and strength for survivors' futures. We will survive!

I also met Shauna Marie MacLean from New Waterford, Nova Scotia, and Jean-Bell Arsenault from Winnipeg, Manitoba – you will read about Shauna and Jean-Bell in separate chapters.

The conference brought together champions and cheerleaders. One champion I had the pleasure of meeting was Leila Springer. We found a few quiet moments to learn about each other and her passion for the cause was evident. Diagnosed with breast cancer in 1999, Leila works tirelessly to help others. She is the co-founder and Executive Director of the Olive Branch of Hope, a breast cancer support group and resource organization in Toronto. Having served on the board of the World Conference on Breast Cancer Foundation for almost two years, Leila has been elected president. She will be the first black woman to lead the WCBCF when the sixth World Conference is held in Hamilton, Ontario, in 2011. I'll definitely be there.

My Six-Month Checkup

*F*all has arrived and so has the appointed time for my six-month post-mastectomy checkup with my surgeon, Dr. Leong. The Toronto air is free of smog today and the sky is crystal clear. My mind is too. This will be a good day. My goal is to leave my doctor's office with absolutely no fear of cancer hanging over my head. I have a very good feeling about this as I walk to Mount Sinai Hospital. I am dripping with positive energy.

My appointment time is 1:45 p.m. and today I decide, at the very least, to attempt to enjoy the ambiance offered to breast cancer survivors at the Marvelle Koffler Breast Centre. This is a wonderful place and I hate it. I hate it because of why I come here. I am grateful to Marvelle Koffler and her family for this wonderful Centre but it does not warm my heart.

There are nine of us waiting today for our appointment time when we will move down the hall and into our privacy cubicle, where we will sit and wait to see our doctor yet again. Until then, we sit quietly, some with a support person by our side. We offer sad but hopeful smiles to each other. We don't invade each other's space. Well, we don't invade each other's space often. On this day, one very elderly lady decides to speak with me. She approaches with a warm and caring smile that makes me smile in return. "Are you the Comfort Heart lady?" she asks as she pulls her Comfort Heart out of her jacket pocket. She has had her Comfort Heart since her cancer journey began, she tells me – nine years and counting without a break – all cancer all the time – and she says this with a determined smile. She is living with cancer and "loves coming to this place" because it feels like home, a much larger home than she lives in. With a sweep of her frail arms she says, "Where else could I go and enjoy such luxurious surroundings with all these people who understand what I am going through?" This angel leaves me with feelings of guilt, and I continue with my quest to see the Marvelle Koffler Breast Centre through a more positive eye.

The furniture here has been very carefully selected and placed to create a warm, almost intimate, atmosphere. I sit in the same copper-coloured fabric chair I seek out each time I am forced to come here: a two-seater in one corner with a beautiful window boasting leaf-like etched glass. Connie and I sat in these very chairs a few months ago. I chose to come alone today to normalize the event. Just in and out for a checkup works best for my mental edge. The sofas are floral with a brown background. The same colour is picked up in the carpet, which is a soft green with copper trim. A portrait of Marvelle Koffler looks out over the room and a book for us to sign sits on a table below the picture. I have never signed the book – it seems like a condolence book to me and I keep that as my private little joke when I see it each time I visit. Not a secret any longer.

The receptionist area of the centre seats two and believe me, these women are kept busy every second of their working shift. We are often a group of upset survivors and we ask these two women a million questions. I believe we are booked three or four at the same time, which really makes things busy when we all arrive, for example, just as these women are finishing their lunch break. We see them coming and we line up on cue. I am booked for 1:45 p.m. and have been here often enough to know that I need to let the 1 p.m. and 1:15 p.m. and 1:30 p.m. survivors line up ahead of me. There is often confusion as more than one survivor tries to understand why she is booked at the same time as the woman lined up in front of her. We can be very fragile on checkup day – often mentally more than physically. Some survivors are very upset while others have been here often enough to understand the drill. That would be me. These receptionists work very very hard and I have the utmost respect for them. They have a big job.

Within the Marvelle Koffler Breast Centre, in Room 1281 you will find Shoppers Home Health Care. I watch women come and go. Many come out with a purchase and a small smile. This Health Care offers sports bras, head scarves and many other items that will make life just a bit easier for a breast cancer survivor. Murray Koffler is the founder of Shoppers Drug Mart so both he and Marvelle have their personal touch evident here.

I have done some work with Shoppers and I like the position they take with the community in terms of giving back. I had the opportunity to speak at three of their conferences in the fall of 2007. Shoppers purchased over 2,000 Comfort Hearts to give out to attendees. Their conference theme was The Human Touch and each time I enter a Shoppers I enjoy their human touch. They practise what they preach. Following my recurrence I visited my local Shoppers often and the pharmacist there, Ravi Chevendra, always took wonderful care of me. He filled my prescriptions but more important he listened to my worries, offered advice when it was appropriate and understood my fear. Never once did Ravi suggest I should not be worried when it appeared that I was overly concerned about my health. I continue to seek him out, even if it is only to say hello.

Things are running a bit late and at 2:10 p.m. I observe a doctor entering our domain. Clearly he is looking for someone. He keeps looking until finally our eyes lock. "He is looking for me," I say under my breath. I am part of a clinical trial and I suspect this doctor wants to take another picture of my chest. I had put him out of my mind after the last picture I posed for. Dr. Alfredo Garcia is part of the investigative study that will offer the "Comparison between 2-octyl-cyanoacrylate tissue adhesive versus sutures in skin closure after breast surgery." That translates to tape versus staples when closing the incision.

I am a great supporter of taking part in clinical trials. It gets you in front of doctors more often in addition to allowing you to be part of a study looking into new procedures, new drugs and/or new methods of doing things. I try to always say "Yes" when asked if I would like to participate in a trial. An informed consent process will take place and it is up to the patient to ask any and all questions you may have prior to making your decision to take part or to refuse to take part in the trial being explained to you. Prior to my birthday surgery I had read and understood the background, purpose, procedure, risks and benefits of this particular trial. I signed up. Today was possibly my last follow-up – and hopefully the last picture that would be taken of my incision-bearing chest.

In this particular trial, tissue adhesives have been studied for over twenty years as an alternative to sutures. My mastectomy incision was closed with a tissue/glue and, honestly, after a day or two I couldn't see any tissue at the incision site at all. It was as if the incision was holding itself together. I didn't like looking at it – it was an excellent incision and the glue worked well, but it was an incision where my breast was supposed to be. When I met with Dr. Garcia I had a tough time answering the question regarding how I felt on a scale of one to ten about the cosmetic look of the incision. I did give it a high rating in the end. My surgeon and my glue worked well together.

When Dr. Garcia finished taking pictures of my scarred chest and asking all of his questions I waited in my little cubicle for Dr. Leong. He arrived only minutes later. I told him immediately that I was here for good news – good news only please. We caught up on a number of things and discussed my health in general. He checked my incision – all was well. Following that, Dr. Leong examined my remaining breast and the underarm lymph node area. Not good. "Have you felt this ridge in your breast?" Dr. Leong softly asked me. "No," I whispered while trying not to puke. The tubular ridge was below the nipple between five and six o'clock. He then examined the lymph node area and found one node that appeared to be enlarged. I was off for a mammogram followed by an ultrasound. Thank God Dr. Leong did not send me home to await a call for these two appointments. I don't think I could have handled a delay of even one day and he seemed to comprehend this just by looking at me. I really like this doctor.

My technologist, Rose, completed the mammogram and asked me to wait outside for my ultrasound. That happened only minutes later and Dr. S. Pantazi, a radiologist, came in to see for herself and to speak with me after the technologist had completed the first round. Dr. Pantazi shared her view that the ridge in my breast appeared to be normal and simply part of my breast tissue. And, that while the node did seem enlarged, all of my nodes appeared to be "plump." Who knew? This might be normal for me too – key word here being "might."

A red flag went up for me during all of this. I had had an MRI a few months ago in July and I don't believe the ridge was there at that time. Where did it come from? Dr. Leong and I agreed that I would come back in six weeks and we would see if there was any change. My appointment was booked and off I went, in a fog of my own.

I left the hospital one more time with the damn cancer cloud hanging over my downcast head. One more time I called my son James with news that came with a "but" attached to it. He has been through so many cancer-related health issues with me. I hate to keep delivering this news to him.

My friend Laura met me at my place later that afternoon. We watched *The Young and the Restless* (yes, it's true, I watch *Y&R*) and then we took ourselves out for dinner. Laura has become a very good friend and even more so since my breast cancer recurrence and during another illness that came my way during this recovery period.

I was one of the unfortunate people who contracted the dreaded listeriosis. Unfortunately for Laura, she was the first person to see me after I spent considerable time on the bathroom floor and even though I warned her in advance that "it's not pretty" I am sure she was a bit shocked when she walked in and saw me. She came with groceries and a plan to get something into my stomach. We tried a bit of ginger ale followed by the tiniest bites of a cracker and then some very plain rice. Initially nothing worked but eventually I was able to eat a bit and from a prone position I watched Laura make jello and more rice for my next day's meal. She threatened to not leave at all if I didn't continue eating while she was in the kitchen. I had to ignore my cancer worries for a few weeks while I dealt with the aftermath of listeriosis. Laura always seems to be near when I need someone to lean on. Her mother died of what began as breast cancer and she was with her mother every step of the way. She is a natural caregiver.

And … six weeks later Laura and I watched *Y&R* again before heading to a Christmas party. I met up with Laura after my follow-up checkup at Mount Sinai.

I have to be honest and say this time I was not at all impressed or pleased with how the receptionist treated me during the check in process. As usual she returned from lunch at 1 p.m. and immediately all of us stood and lined up to check in. I am sure this is a terrible process for her to manage. The first woman in line was not a 1 p.m.

check in. (It may have been her first time so she did not know the routine.) She was told to let the 1 p.m. appointments check in first and she stepped out of line with a defeated look on her face. I bet she came early enough to ensure she was first in line. The receptionist seemed frustrated with us and abruptly told us she would call out the 1 p.m. appointments rather than have us line up. She called and processed four survivors; my name did not come up. I was a 1 o'clocker according to my note from Dr. Leong's office. When she announced she would now call the 1:15 p.m. appointments I stepped forward and said I had a 1 p.m. appointment. In a not-too-soft voice and without eye contact she told me, "I have already called *all* of the 1 p.m. appointments and you did not step up." As she began to process someone else I put my piece of paper in front of her. She looked at the form and, again without eye contact, said, "You do not have an appointment for today. I will have to deal with this. Take a seat."

For those who know me well you will be surprised that this treatment brought tears to my eyes. Something this small was huge for me in the moment. I sat down where she could easily see me because I didn't want her to forget I was standing by. I heard her call Betty at my surgeon's office and within minutes all was cleared up. I was processed and sent to the clinic where I was first-up to see Dr. Leong. I was immediately examined by a doctor new to me who, like Dr. Leong, has strong people skills.

Dr. Vivian Yuen examined my breast and the lymph node area that had been the problem six weeks ago and shared further details from the ultrasound with me. The breast issue was cleared up in that the ridge found was indeed part of my breast tissue. It had not been highlighted following my earlier MRI because it was not a hot spot. Cancer would be the hot spot. The node that was enlarged six weeks ago was no longer enlarged – all was well. Except, I then had to tell Dr. Yuen that since seeing Dr. Leong the last time I had found another lump. This one was on my back. Here we go again.

Dr. Leong joined us and after confirming that all breast issues were now resolved and I would be booked for a follow-up appointment in six months, he examined the lump I brought with me today. It was agreed that I would have a needle biopsy and could expect pathology results in a couple of weeks. I would also be booked for an ultrasound but it would not be today. I was in the breast clinic for my checkup with Dr. Leong and this was no longer a breast issue.

I left Mount Sinai almost wishing I had not found the lump on my back. I had so hoped I could end the year with a total clean bill of health, with not one single cancer-related health issue. This may not be cancer but when a cancer survivor is in a cancer clinic and pathology is needed to confirm that a lump is not cancer, we worry. I am sick and tired of calling my son with shaky news. It is what it is — today is December 4, 2008, and I want this to be over before year's end.

I do not wait well for test results and this time I needed to do something rather than wait over the holiday season. I contacted Dr. Tannenbaum, who saw me on December 9 and said he would try to get pathology results for me as soon as possible. He did exactly that. One day later he contacted me with good news. The tumour was a benign lipoma and not a worry at all. I would see Dr. Tannenbaum in a few months and he would check the tumour again at that time. I did tuck away in the back of my mind the ultrasound that Dr. Leong had ordered. Ideally, the ultrasound would simply be confirmation of the good news.

Rather than feeling total excitement and the desire to do the victory dance, I felt kind of numb with this news. I couldn't and can't explain why I felt this way. The numbness lasted for a day or so and then I began to celebrate. Finally, my six-month checkup was over (at this stage who cares if it took nine months?) and it appeared that all was well. No more cancer. I could hardly believe it. It had been a long year for me and for my family, from January 3 to December 10. I can say, "I am cancer free" once again. I plan to say, "I am cancer free" for at least another sixteen years. I am off to live my life.

James, Tracey and Jalen made plans to visit me the following day. We have much to celebrate.

Jean-Bell Arsenault – Dancing in the Rain

I met Jean-Bell at the World Conference on Breast Cancer, and as we began to learn more about each other via e-mail in the weeks that followed, I asked her to journal her story. Here is what she wrote.

Paul and I had a dream. We would retire early and winter somewhere in a warm climate. Manitoba winters can be pretty severe. A few years before retirement and through Paul's work we had lived in Africa for a period of seven years. We got used to the year-round summer months and we truly loved it. After retirement we headed for Texas, where we had friends who wintered there, and in time we purchased a little home. We were known as Winter Texans. It was wonderful to be able to go south for five months every winter. We had the best of both worlds and I thought we were spoiled by the great life we were leading. Things began to change.

I found a dry spot on my face near the nose – it was growing. My doctor arranged for surgery and sure enough it was skin cancer. This was the first time the word cancer was uttered in our family. Sort of scary but after reading all about skin cancer I did feel better. I have fair skin and always had lots of freckles when I was young. I got through this and accepted it as part of my life. Paul and I have always been positive in everything we did or everything that came into our life. We continued our travelling when the seasons changed. Two years later this spot came back and this time my doctor had a plastic surgeon take a larger spot out – same thing

– skin cancer. I do heal fast and this new doctor told me the spot would never come back. And it never did.

The following year Paul had quite a large spot removed from his back – melanoma. This was not good. Once again we read everything we could about melanoma and this helped us get through this latest scare.

For years I had been experiencing a breast problem called fibrocystic breast disease. Lots of bump and lump biopsies over the years. I had a wonderful surgeon, Dr. G, who saw me every six months and took very good care of me. He told me to stop taking anything with caffeine in it. He biopsied every one of these lumps and the results came back negative. Life was good.

In 2004 I went for my usual mammogram before we headed south. Something was not right. Dr. G sent me for a CAT scan and sure enough there was something suspicious. I had to have another biopsy. The results came the day I went to have the stitches removed. When Dr. G said the words "breast cancer" it took my breath away. I felt I could not breathe. I kept thinking that this happened to other people but not to me. No, not me. My results were always negative, or they had been until now. A surgery date was set and I was off to see an oncologist. I felt fortunate that it was the same oncologist Paul saw every six months.

We made a fast trip down south to sell our winter home and to bring our personal belongings back with us. We had a wonderful eleven years travelling south for the winters and were happy to have so many new friends that we will never forget. We had nothing to complain about.

We had six children, one deceased now, and we have quite a few grandchildren. We have forever been a very close family. Someone is always making a get-together for some reason. Sometimes there is no reason at all; we just want to be near each other. I think the hardest thing was to call each of our children and have to tell them this news. To hear the words cancer and Mom in the same sentence was devastating to them. I knew there would be a lot of support when I needed it. And there would always be someone for me to talk to – my family would be there. Paul was my rock every day. He spoiled me constantly. My daughter Wendy made arrangements to take me to a breast cancer support group meeting in our town.

Paul, Wendy, and our number four son, Bruce, came with me to this meeting. As we were walking in to the meeting Bruce said, "Mom, if I hear one negative word, I'm taking you out of here." It was funny because some of the ladies heard him and they were quick to say there would be no negative words spoken here. This meeting and these ladies were the best thing for me. They had all been through what I was about to go through. They helped me so much. The next morning there was a bouquet of pink tulips delivered from the group. They also brought me books to read and tapes to listen to. Friends are angels who lift us to our feet when our wings have trouble remembering how to fly. To this day I attend their monthly meetings and help out where I can. There is always someone who has breast cancer who needs help.

The surgery went well, as Dr. G put it. There were no cancer cells in the lymph nodes. I was put on Arimidex for at least five years. We once again read everything we could get our hands on about breast cancer. Paul was such a rock in my life now. When I came home from the hospital he took over all the cooking and tidying up. Always there with hugs when I needed them and a shoulder when I needed to rant or cry. This cancer is another bead on my string and I'll wear it all my life. Each bead is a precious reminder of an unforgettable lesson in living and in my life. There is life after cancer … I was getting stronger every day. I was really trying to feel positive every day. Some days were not good but not many of those any more. My granddaughter Rhonda came to see me one day and told me she envisioned Grampa and me living to be 110 years old, and dying in bed together. I liked that and we are both going to do our best to carry that out.

I was healing slowly. My oncologist told us I needed radiation. When I was at the hospital getting my little tattoos and having everything set up for radiation, a CAT scan showed something on my lung. My doctor called me in. For now, the radiation was cancelled. I had to be booked for other tests – priorities change. An appointment was made and tests were done with a cardiovascular and thoracic surgeon. She put the scans up on the machine to show us what she was seeing – not good. There was a 5-centimetre (2-inch) goober on my lung that did not belong there. This was two months since the breast surgery and I was devastated with this news as were Paul and our children. I want to wake up every morning with Paul, I want to live to be 110 years old and I want to see my great-grandchildren grow up – for a little while at least.

The bronchoscope showed nothing as the goober was too far down in my lung. Surgery was scheduled for two weeks later. Everything was moving so fast. The lung surgery was three months exactly after my breast *surgery. When I woke from my fuzzy state my family was all around me. "Is it cancer?" I asked, but I already knew the answer. I felt like a stuffed teddy that had all the stuffing knocked out of her. Double kick in the gut. That's for sure. That night I woke up about 4 a.m. I guess everything started to sink in, and I started to cry, not because I was feeling sorry for myself, but because I had always been the strong one. I was always the keeper of our children and Paul. I was always in charge of my body; now I had no control at all. I had to lie on my back constantly. I remember my tears were running into my ears. A nurse came in and sat with me, holding my hand and wiping my tears. Where did this angel come from when I needed her at 4 a.m.? She told me this was a natural reaction.*

The surgeon had to take the lower lobe of the right lung, and some lymph nodes. She told me I would be sore for six months or more as she had to cut some of the nerves out plus had to crack or break some ribs. Can there be good news here? Yes, there was. There were no cancer cells in the lymph nodes, thank goodness. They also found that this cancer was not metastasized from the breast. So I had two primary cancers. I didn't know if that's good or bad.

Three days later Wendy came to visit with Rhonda and her two wee babies. Jubilee sat beside me being so very careful not to hurt Nana. Here we were four generations of me: Jean-Bell, Wendy Jean, Rhonda Jean, Jubilee Jean three years old and baby Nova Jens only one year old. When they left I cried with Paul. My family is so special to me. That day was the best.

The day I found out I had breast cancer I started a journal. I found I could pour all my feelings in there. I would advise anyone going through a dramatic time to journal. I am in to my second journal now and it has been a big help to me. It helped when I wanted to rant and rave and when I was in pain. When I came home from the lung surgery I wanted my body and my mind to be quiet and rested.

What is my God thinking? He meant for us to sleep at night. Every pain is worse at night. Every worry is larger at night. My oncologist had given me something for the pain. It did not help. Later she gave me morphine – what a blessing that was. It would help for a few hours at a time. Paul had to help me to bed and to get me up like I was a little baby. Everyone should have a Paul like mine. Someone had to bathe me and wash my hair. For a while I felt totally useless.

We have always lived in the country and we loved it. We were about an hour away from the city and when this illness happened we talked about moving into an apartment in the city one of these years. Paul wanted this to happen now so I could be closer to the doctors and hospitals. A move to the city. What would I do without my garden, fresh tomatoes and vegetables, and all my flowers? Where would we sit in the morning to have our coffee if we had no deck? We did it. We picked out an apartment with a big balcony for my flowers and for me and we were seven floors up above all the trees. Our kids all came and helped Paul paint, polish and go through everything so we could downsize. The house sold almost right away. The move was on. I couldn't do much at all, except designate jobs and tell everyone what to do. Our kids were all there through that big move, doing everything for me. What angels. It took a while but I have gotten used to apartment and city living. I can grow fresh tomatoes and herbs on my balcony after all.

Six months after the breast surgery my radiation began. With freckles and fair skin I burned and blistered pretty badly. I had twenty-five treatments. When it was over we took our camper to the woods to be away from doctors and treatments. We walked, read, meditated and talked. We talked about how fortunate I really was with the past year behind me. I was in pretty good shape, still pretty sore but that too would get better. Now I was on a program of laughter and vitamin C. I was exactly where I was meant to be. I was focused on meditation, relaxing, resting, and lots of positive thinking. With Paul, my family and my support group I would heal and make all of this a memory.

The next year was wonderful. I was getting my strength back fast and felt just great. How good is life. Never underestimate the power of positive thinking.

Right after the New Year a routine CAT scan was done and a small lump was found in the same lung but at the top of the lung this time. This was so small the lung surgeon told us we would wait and see how fast it grew, if it grew at all. After another scan a couple of months later we learned that this new thing was growing, but very slowly. The surgeon didn't want to take the rest of the lung out if we could avoid it, and the oncologist said we should leave it alone. I felt okay with this decision. That day I went out and bought myself flowers. Fresh flowers are a necessity sometimes, not a frill. Cancer has made me so much stronger. There's a saying, "That which doesn't kill me, makes me strong."

Our daughter Wendy has been having trouble with her breast; she also has fibrocystic breast disease. She has had a few lumps removed and, of course, this is a worry at first and for a brief minute or two there was guilt because I have passed this on to her. No. I passed on something of me that's great to all of my children – my spirit and positive attitude. We found out Wendy has what is called "atypical hyperplasia," benign but this does increase the risk of breast cancer.

The next CAT scan shows the goober in my lung is still growing slowly. The big "but" is that there is something growing around it – a shadow or a film surrounding it. Life isn't about waiting for the storm to pass; it's about learning to dance in the rain. And I'm certainly not waiting for this storm to pass. I'm dancing, I'm dancing!

My lung surgeon said if she removed the rest of the lung I may not survive the surgery. If they leave it alone there is a chance it may spread through the lymph nodes or the blood to other parts of the body (metastasis). I found out the growing tumour in my lung is cancer, and what is growing around it is called "ground glass" in lung cancer. On the CAT scan it looks just like ground or tiny bits of broken glass. It refers to the presence of increased hazy opacity lesions (more cancer) and in some cases can be operated on.

I, along with my family and surgeon, decided there will be no surgery on the lung. I'm going to stay happy and positive, do the things I want to do and try to finish my "bucket list." Yes, I have one of those and am having a fun time planning the next thing to cross off the list. We are going to plant a "love" tree and then we're heading on a trip to the east coast with some of the family. More things to cross off my list. Four years ago when the cancer attacked me I took up painting. I have quite a few pictures finished and want to complete a few more. I wanted to tell my cancer story and now, thanks to Carol Ann encouraging me, this too is something I can cross off my list.

God whispers to our souls and to our hearts. Sometimes when we don't take the time to listen He throws a brick at us. It's our choice to listen to the whisper or wait for the brick. I certainly don't want the brick. I'm listening for the whisper.

I'm so happy and satisfied with my life. Paul and I go to movies, visit our children often, go for walks, go out for dinners together, go to church, and go camping in the woods and meditate.

A family is a circle of love and strength. Every joy shared adds more love. Every obstacle faced together makes the circle stronger.

What's in store for me and my family? Only God knows the answer to this question and we will let Him decide. In the meantime, we will go on living the way we have … one day at a time.

Jean-Bell and I will continue to stay in touch as she works on her bucket list and enjoys life with her family. I am very proud of her.

Carol Anne Krupicz –
Cancer and Life After Retirement

*C*arol Anne and I share a name, a career with Bell and a cancer history. Her story resonates with me on many levels. She is a very strong lady.

I dedicate these two stories to my husband, Stan, and to my parents, who have always been here for me. Also, to my twin sister Teresa and my Aunt Victoria. I love all of you dearly. And I want to thank Carol Ann Cole, who has given me the opportunity to express my feelings in her book.

Second Chance:
My feelings when I found out I had cancer in January 1996

Sometimes in life, God gives us a second chance – grab that rainbow. When you hear that someone you know has cancer, you think, "I will never get it."

Do not take life for granted, as it can be cut short in seconds. When I was told I had ovarian cancer I thought, "You must have the wrong person." I always took care of myself, ate well, and did not abuse my body. At first when I was told, my doctor asked, "Are you okay?" It did not register. Thoughts came into my mind: Who do I call? What about my girls and my life? Why is God punishing me? I was a good Catholic. I had gone through so many hardships in my life already: the loss of a baby daughter, a marriage that failed, trying to be a good mother and raising two daughters on my own.

After the initial shock, I had decisions to make: telling my family, surgery and the possibility of treatments. Weeks before, I had a checkup and all was fine. The next month was so trying. I had ovarian cancer, a fast-growing cancer which doctors said if not caught in time could be fatal. Surgery was elected and my gynaecologist decided it would be laser surgery. Unfortunately, this was not an option as the tumour was encased around the ovaries. Major surgery was done and pathologists at Sunnybrook Cancer Hospital in Toronto said it was a malignant tumour. Weeks later, I was told the grim news that a second surgery had to be performed and I had to have a complete hysterectomy. It was a rough recovery as infection set in. Then my Aunt Victoria and I travelled for many months to Sunnybrook Cancer Hospital. Without her, I do not know how I would have done it. One of the oncologists we saw indicated that I was one lucky lady, especially with the type of cancer I had.

There were times when I felt down and depressed, but when I saw some patients at the hospital, I felt lucky and thanked God for giving me a second chance. Going through my surgeries, I was mad at the world as I knew I was young and would never be able to have any more children. At the same time, I was grateful that I was alive.

When people learn you have cancer, they think you have the plague. I found some family members would not talk about it, and friends and co-workers who I was close to at Bell Canada were afraid to come visit or call. During the months of my recovery, I think I tried to block out the word cancer to the point of not letting my twin sister Teresa into my life, afraid that she could get it. Doctors at Sunnybrook helped me with a therapist, Dr. J. Moss, who I am grateful to to this day. People dealing with cancer feel alone during both good and bad times. I hit rock bottom, even though the cancer was caught. Then one day something clicked in my mind as if a little voice was saying, HELLO. WAKE UP AND SMELL THE COFEEE. YOU ARE ALIVE. I started to realize that all these months of not allowing Teresa, Bell co-workers and friends to help and to be there for me was a huge mistake.

Once I opened my heart, everyone could not do enough. They helped organize a food drive – enough food to last a year. My sister wanted to do anything she could. In a time like this, a person dealing with cancer needs *help. Accept the help; let people do little things from picking up a maga-zine for you, to buying groceries, or even visiting. They want to enjoy your company and be there for you. Never mind what you look like; they do not care about your looks. It's what's inside that counts.*

I have come to realize being faced with cancer has changed my life in such a good way. To me, life is precious and we need to stop and smell the flowers, look at the blue skies. You really look at things and people dif-ferently. Even your enemies are no longer your enemies. The little things are not important. If you did not dust the furniture today, who cares? Through my strong belief in the Catholic faith, I was able to overcome my fears and deal with my sickness.

I thank God every day for giving me a second chance at life.

Stan really believes that we were put together by God for a rea-son. We both went through cancer in different ways. Stan's first wife suc-cumbed to the illness and then he was with me through mine. He under-stands what a person goes through. We met at a dinner theatre and he truly is my soulmate, as he makes me laugh every day. He has such a zest for life and wants to live life to the fullest with me. People do not need mon-ey or riches to be happy. You need someone to love, share your life whether in good or bad times. It is very lonely to be by yourself looking at four walls. You need to be there for each other every day. Memories that two people share are so important and you should never lose sight of them. My husband loves to make me laugh and he is so thoughtful in his own way. When we got engaged he put the ring on the telephone cord as he knew I would see it when I needed to answer the telephone. I also inherited a stepson, David, who is a chip off the block. When we got married he gave a speech indicating I was good to him. He calls me his surrogate mom.

Even though I was faced with cancer, I do not dwell upon it. I try to do something nice for myself everyday whether it is reading, buying an ice cream or making a point to have lunch with Teresa or friends. Be thankful that you wake up each morning and can face another day. I am also grate-ful I am happy and enjoying life with my husband and that we can still travel, spend time with family and friends.

Life after Bell

After dealing with cancer, retirement should have come easily to me but it didn't. Retirement to me seemed like a death sentence. Here I was fifty-one years of age and thirty-three years of service with Bell Canada, a job which was my whole life. I was too young. Retirement was for people in their seventies. My mind was spinning. What was I going to do after Bell? Could I make a go of it? Would I be able to live on my pension? I still had one daughter left to put through school.

Leaving a job I loved, friends and co-workers – I was not ready to leave this chapter of my life. Many of us were offered packages and a decision had to be made within a month. This was not picking out paint colours; it was a decision I would have to live with the rest of my life. I seemed to be sitting on a fence being pushed one way or another. Lots of sleepless nights but the countdown was on. Part of me felt that Bell was pushing us older people out after so many years.

My family did not want me to retire, even though they never said it in so many words. I think to them, this meant they were getting older. Our financial advisor said it was a go after reviewing the package. My husband Stan was so supportive as we mulled over the possibility of retirement. In both of our minds, we had not thought that retirement was an option. We were set financially; it was the idea that I was only fifty-one. To our surprise, we had more pros than cons to consider.

The upside to retirement included no more travelling for those early hours at work, or late hours getting home, savings on gas, clothes, lunches, parking and car insurance, and the freedom to enjoy life. The downside to retirement meant not seeing co-workers and friends daily.

When the decision was finally made and papers signed for the end of the year, it felt as if a weight was lifted off my shoulders. There would be no turning back. As the year and my career at Bell Canada ended, one chapter of my life closed and another one was about to open.

Taking retirement for me has opened many doors. One rule of thumb that I have heard from many people including Stan is that you must keep busy. Now I am able to do things I was never able to do when I was at the office. When they are working, people tend to say they will do it tomorrow, but they never get around to it. With retirement, I can do the things I always wanted to explore. My husband took early retirement and has kept busy over the years with his family farm doing gardening of flowers and vegetables. He says it is not a chore but a pleasure, going with his brothers sometimes weekly and puttering around in the gardens.

At first when I retired, it took some months to adjust. I got involved in quilting, both machine and hand, as I had sewed for years. I completed a queen-size comforter and table runners. My friends and family were so impressed that I ended up giving them away for gifts. I am now in the midst of completing more quilted runners with the cancer wordings and emblems which have a special meaning to me. My husband got involved in helping me with the cutting out in my quilting projects so it turned out to be a joint venture. This meant we were able to spend more quality time together. I may even give them to the church for a well-known cause.

Retirement has given us more time to travel around the world together and spend more time with my parents, especially my twin sister Teresa. We were estranged for many years. Retirement has given me the opportunity to do so much and enjoy life to the fullest, especially with those people I love.

May Ocean – CHO (Comfort Heart Owner)

I have great admiration for strong-willed, determined and intelligent women. May Ocean is all of those. She is my business partner as it relates to my fundraiser and she is my friend. This is her story.

The decision to change my name took place while in divorce court. When it came time to discuss and sign the documents I was simply asked if I wanted to change my name. I picked up on the fact that I was not specifically asked if I wanted to go back to my maiden name. I asked if it was okay to select any name of my own choosing. I was told it was definitely okay and it was also mentioned that within the realm of divorce, this would be free. Otherwise, to change one's name would cost around $500.

I had to decide right there and then on a name. After only a moment of thought, I chose Ocean. When I was about five or six years of age, my siblings and I were told stories about my mother and father's family in Canada (we were living in Germany at the time) and I was most impressed with stories about the ocean. I had never seen the ocean before but I thought it must be like the biggest swimming pool ever.

When I would get together with my cousins, aunts and uncles and especially my grandmother for the first time, I became aware of a larger community of family love. And in the backyard lay the most magnificent and beautiful thing I had ever seen – the ocean. I built many a sandcastle there amidst scurrying sandpipers and the little birds that tunnelled out nests along the low-lying cliffs of the shore's edge. I would explore the shores for miles and for many a summer after that, I would swim in the endless salt waters. My cousins, and there were many, my little sister Linda and I would swim out as far as we could with wooden lobster traps that we had borrowed from our uncle. I would always swim my trap out farther than anyone else. I was a good strong swimmer and I knew that the farther out I could set the trap, the better chance there was of catching a few lobsters instead of only crabs. We would have beach parties at night, feasting on our catch.

As the years went by, the ocean would always be a place where I would return ... not only for fun and holiday, but for solitude and solace. It is funny to think that the ocean is where I feel most grounded. So, as you can see, it was not hard for me to know just exactly what my new name should be.

Interestingly enough, my name and the word "may" come down to our day and age from the Old English word magan, the Old Icelandic mega, and Proto-Germanic root mag, originally meaning "might." The silent letter g used to be pronounced as a hard k in days of old. (In fact, all words of today that contain ght were originally pronounced as k.) I guess that is why we can say either I may or I might. Until recently, I never realized that my full name is really Mighty Ocean ... and so perhaps the name had really chosen me instead of the other way around. Call me a romantic if you like, but I like to think of it all as a special gift from our mothers – the sacrifices and struggles they have made throughout time to bring balance.

And so, when we met in the mid '90s she was May Ocean.

While working for a large pewter company, May knew her values were vastly different from those of her bosses. She left – with her two young children in hand. She bought a building, built an apartment on the top floor to house herself, Chris and Erin, and she launched OceanArt Pewter in White's Lake, Nova Scotia. The name of her business comes as no surprise.

May's storefront carried, in a wicker basket at the cash, tiny pewter Worry Hearts and I fell in love with them the moment I saw them. Over time, and working with May and her sister, Linda Power, the Worry Hearts became Comfort Hearts and the Comfort Heart Initiative was born.

There is a very personal connection to cancer for May. When we met, Linda had already battled cancer twice and May was proud to share that she had been looking for the right way to become involved in the raising of funds for cancer research. This seemed like the perfect fit for May and for her company. Even though OceanArt Pewter was not a huge financial success, May was quick to agree to give up her net proceeds on sales of all Comfort Hearts. It was not then, and it is not now, about the money for May.

May would agree there were times when she did not hire her staff based on a required skill set or the need for an additional employee. If a single mother approached May and said, "I am desperate and I need a job" not much else was asked; the job was created if one did not exist. Sometimes it worked and sometimes it did not. In recent years May closed her major storefronts and now operates a smaller OceanArt Pewter. With a hands-on approach May and Denise Sooley, who has been working with May for many years, personally make and package every Comfort Heart we need.

In the early years of my fundraiser I went to a Christmas party in Kentville, Nova Scotia, with May. She attended the party held to thank her team working in the Kentville store in the Annapolis Valley. Her friend Cathy came with us too. En route back to Halifax, May began what was a very long story. She kept saying, "I want to share something with you" but then she would skirt (pun intended) around the issue. Finally she said, "Cathy and I want you to know we are gay – we are partners. Are you okay with that?" When I told them that this was not news to me and May asked, "How did you know?" I quietly said, "It's not complicated, May. I just knew." Nothing else needed to be said. We were totally comfortable with this and with our friendship. Friends forever.

May has said that at one point she thought she would never see a time when being gay was acceptable. People have an amazing propensity for growth and a great ability to turn around from their prejudices and preconceived notions. Some are slower than others to make this leap and May is looking forward to the day when everyone who knows her will judge her for the person she is, not her sexual orientation. She is looking forward to the day when every gay man and woman is given this freedom.

The artist in May is clearly evident in her description of a dream she had about our friend Doctor Annie Smith, PhD, who lost her courageous battle with cancer. "Shortly after Annie died, I had a dream about her. I was going through a very unsettling time regarding her death. The dream was odd – short and simple, but what is important is how it made me feel. In my dream, we were on a big wide open lake and she was taking me out for a drive in a small speedboat which she had at full throttle. We were flying and she was so happy – freedom and wind in her hair. With one hand on the wheel and beaming with pride, she put her other arm around my shoulder. Her look clearly said, 'Don't worry, May. I'm very happy.' It was an odd dream because, as everyone knows, Annie was into sailing and canoeing, but then dreams are more about symbolism. Even though I don't understand the symbolism, I understand the emotion. Annie is happy, and for some unexplainable reason, I now feel sure of this. There are things that science and rationale can never fully explain – things of the heart. Four is half of eight in the mathematical sense, but three is half of eight in the artsy heart sense. There is much more to life than what meets the eye. Annie was so much more."

I have an original piece of art by Doctor Annie. Hanging proudly on my wall beside my Order of Canada certificate is my Order of the Heart certificate created by Annie with her trademark bear front and centre. A wonderful group of friends (mostly from my Bell days) presented the framed certificate to me, signed by all, just days before my trip to Ottawa to receive the Order of Canada. I met Annie for the first time that evening and shortly after we met she contacted me to explore the possibility of being introduced to May. She was interested in having pewter bears made that she could sell with proceeds going to ovarian cancer research and was hopeful that May could create the bear pin for her. Introductions were made and the pewter bear was created. Many an evening we all sat in Annie's tiny Toronto apartment packaging the Annie bears over wine and scotch. Lots of wine and scotch.

On Halloween 2007 Annie Bear, or Doctor Bear as she was affectionately known, passed away. She set sail with all of her cancer gremlins set free at last. Annie was an alumnus of Wellesley College, Stanford University and the University of Toronto, where she earned her PhD. She was justifiably proud of her role in founding the Art and Art History Program at Sheridan College. The Annie Smith Arts

Centre at Sheridan is a tribute to Annie's influence in the field of education. She was an outstanding, innovative teacher and, for me, the ultimate example of one who really understands the difference between the certificate on the wall and the soft skills that can truly touch others. Annie knew how to do that.

After Doctor Annie passed away, May shared with me that she had lots of Annie's bear products in stock at OceanArt pewter. We will find the right home for every bear and keep her memory alive. We are not alone. In December 2008 I was honoured to speak about "Reflections of Annie" at the annual Holly Bear Tennis Tournament, now in Annie's memory, held at the Toronto Lawn Tennis Club. Over $10,000 was raised in a few short hours to support the Annie Bear Fund for Ovarian Cancer at Princess Margaret Hospital. Some of the money came from the sale of Annie's original bear drawings and from her personal bear collection. The event was so personal it sometimes felt that Annie would walk into the room at any time. Annie was a long-time member of the club and she will be remembered there forever. We cried and we laughed as we honoured our friend.

May has a new joy in her life, a granddaughter and her first grandchild. Addisyn will come to love the ocean as much as her wonderful Mamere (Acadian for Nana). We will introduce Addisyn to Jalen one day. I pray that in their lifetime there will be a cure for cancer and they will wonder what the Comfort Heart project was all about way back in the early 2000s.

I will be forever grateful to May for her own generous heart all those years ago when I first approached her with my idea to raise money for cancer research through the sale of the pewter heart she created. The thumb imprint you will find in your Comfort Heart belongs to May. I consider it her stamp of approval.

Cecelia May Parker –
With a Higher Power on Her Shoulder

Cecelia May Parker could have a chip on her shoulder rather than a higher power, but she chooses to live her life looking forward, not back. She asks for help when she needs it, leans on friends and family when that works best and she gets on with her life. We have lots in common, including the fact that we are cousins and we are breast cancer survivors. I am very proud of my cousin. This is her personal story.

On February 7, 2003, I was diagnosed with breast cancer. When I found the lump, somehow I knew the diagnosis would be breast cancer – I just knew. The lump was situated below the nipple in the right breast. I could actually see the lump sitting under the skin. "Come and get me."

Thanks to my family doctor I was not forced to stress for a long time waiting for test results and surgery. I had the tumour removed in March. I maintained a very positive mindset. I researched the type of cancer I had: estrogen positive with HER2/nue positive cells – nine of them. I was told I was unique in that only 20 percent of women in North America have this cell. I can't explain why, but I was calm. My support system was in place. My friends stepped up. I had a support group that I went to once a week and a great therapist who I could talk to at any time. I learned to release by hitting a pillow, screaming into a towel, in the car or in the shower. I allowed myself to cry whenever I felt the need. Carol Ann calls that a pity party and it worked for me.

I prioritized my journey. I called the removal of the cancerous tumour my Phase One. I did not allow myself to feel depressed for very long. I was going to live. My mindset as such that when the tumour was removed I no longer had cancer. Everything that was to happen from then on was prevention so the cancer would not return.

After removal of the tumour I did lots of different exercises. The pain subsided very quickly. My range of motion as a result of exercising was not limited at all. Everything was working as it should.

In April I was told that I would have to endure chemo, four sessions followed by radiation. My cancer had been Grade 3 and so these aggressive treatments were essential to my case. My chemo was my Phase Two.

I was assigned to the same oncologist Carol Ann had years ago, Dr. Martin Blackstein, and I could immediately appreciate why she sang his praises so much. Dr. Blackstein told me everything I needed to know about the type of chemo I was to have and why. I sat listening to him very calmly and asked him to write down the names of every single chemical that would be forced into my body to kill any cancer residue. I asked about the amount of each chemical I would receive and why I would take these particular drugs. The more I knew the more empowered I felt. I could do this.

I went home and researched all of the drugs.

The infusion lasted for three and one-half hours. Some days it felt like a lifetime. I lost my hair two weeks and one day after my first infusion. I was in the shower and out it came. Rather than feel sorry for myself I actually found it helped me become a stronger woman. A friend came over and helped me remove all of the remaining clumps of hair that stuck stubbornly to my half-bald head. Hair grows back and I took the stand that this was the least of my worries. Living was my priority.

When I was scheduled to have my second infusion I was told it had to be delayed. My white cell count was too low – panic for me. Had I done something to cause this? Was I somehow preventing myself from taking treatment that would help me get better? My nurses assured me this happens sometimes and it was not my fault. The bone marrow which reproduces white cells acts slower in some people. I was one of those people. After that experience, rather than prepare me for the infusion each time, they waited for blood results first. I was thankful for this. Having the needles inserted and removed with no treatment was tough. Each time I had a needle inserted there was lots of bruising and I didn't need to be poked unnecessarily.

My chemotherapy experience made me stronger. Even though I was sick after every single treatment I knew that I was going to get through this experience. And I did.

My Phase Three was radiation – another prevention procedure. I found radiation to be necessary but also a huge loss of time. You need a very short amount of time for the actual radiation but each day was a long day. Each day I was scheduled for a different time and some days the treatment was cancelled at the last minute due to machine malfunction. It was impossible to plan even a day, not to mention my life. I found this frustrating and beyond my control.

Phase Four – Herceptin. Because I had the HER2/nue receptors which were positive I was asked to participate in the Hera Study. Herceptin is a drug that fights the HER2/nue specifically. I joined the trial but was not given the drug until one year after finishing both chemo and radiation. During the trial I received a placebo, not the actual drug. As soon as Herceptin was approved I began receiving it.

I held the belief that whatever was out there that would help me survive was what I would do or take. I also started taking tamoxifen after chemo and radiation.

When people, especially other cancer survivors, ask me how I got thrugh this life-threatening experience I am happy to tell them. I stayed focused on being positive as much as I could. I researched everything that went into my body or was done to my body and I had a strong support system in place. I took good care of myself and I believed in a higher power sitting on my shoulder. I put myself first.

Empowerment. Knowledge. Strength. Belief. Research. Questioning everything that was happening to me. Believing that once the cancerous tumour was surgically removed from my body I could relax because I would then know I no longer had cancer. This all worked for me.

The experience made me who I am today – a much stronger woman. Perhaps it was meant to be. Life is always a struggle with challenges placed in our path. I have had my share of challenges and cancer was only one of them. My life journey is not over – and I am thankful for this.

I hope that by reading my story in Carol Ann's book someone will learn from my experience and how I handled it. If even one woman becomes more positive after reading my story, I will consider that a gift.

Mary Rose Cole (d'Entremont)

*I*continue to be influenced by my mother and I continue to learn from her so many years after her death. During my Bell career it was common knowledge that I was attached at the hip to my filofax and when Mom moved in with me prior to her death she shared her own filofax of sorts. Her little black book (literally a little black book) was titled CSD – sterilization procedure for trays. Mom began working outside of the home in her fiftieth year and following her first job in the laundry department of the Halifax Infirmary she was promoted to CSD – Central Sterilization Department. This was Mom's "big job at the Infirmary" as evidenced in the notes she kept, and as remembered by the women she trained on the job. My "big job at the Bell" paled by comparison in many ways.

Mom's black book contained details relative to every tray and associated tool she would sterilize for doctors' and nurses' use. She kept specific notes about doctors who liked things in his or her own way. Mom was expected to know all levels of detail. Additionally, she kept notes about what was expected of her over and above the norm when working the night shift and how the 7 a.m. shift should begin each day.

With great pride Mom showed me her job description dated April 12, 1977. She had been transferred within departments at the Infirmary to become a CSD aide and, with good performance, could be promoted to supervisor. Her job description was noted formally as, "Cleans, sterilizes, and assembles equipment, supplies and instruments according to prescribed procedures and techniques." The job description went on to explain requirements for aptitude, interests, temperament, physical demands and working conditions. Mom met all requirements.

It was in this job that Mom met the sisters, as she would refer to them over the years – five sisters to be exact, who would become good friends both on and off the job. Mom worked with Melva and Betty first and then Natalie came on board. Mom was assigned to help Natalie learn the job and her friendship with this wonderful family grew. There were two more sisters – Audrey and Rosalie. Mom and Rosalie shared the same birthday, December 22, and each year all six would get together to celebrate Christmas and their birthday.

I remember so fondly one trip Mom and I made to Halifax. I had not yet met her friends. It was a sunny summer day and we were walking on the boardwalk along the harbour enjoying the sights. Suddenly we heard, "Mary, is that you?" followed by laughing and hugs all around. Mom quickly introduced me and then suggested I could go on ahead while she visited with the sisters. She would meet me later at the hotel. I felt dismissed but in a good way. Mom could not wait to catch up with her friends and they had so much to talk about.

Mom would be pleased that her own daughters have since formed a close bond with her friends from CSD. When JohnD, Connie's husband, was in the hospital with his first cancer surgery we reconnected with Melva, who was working on the floor where John would stay during his recovery. Meeting Melva's four sisters again soon followed. We keep Mom's memory alive. I try to visit the girls in their Halifax home each time I visit Nova Scotia and we speak on the phone. When I call, I never know which of the five sisters I am speaking with. I think they enjoy confusing me.

These five sisters could teach others so much about respecting and being loyal to family. They purchased a home together, one that they are very proud of. Over time some of them and all of them have lived together in their home. They care very deeply for each other and do so many little things to make life a bit easier for each other. They maintain a taxi fund so when one is working late there is money for a taxi rather than having to take the bus home after dark. When one of the girls takes on an extra responsibility (putting out the garbage, for example) there is an extra gift of thanks under the Christmas tree. And they never feel a need to do everything together. Those who like bingo go to bingo and those who like to dine out do exactly that. They tell some very funny stories about not being intimidated when dining in the ultra high-end restaurants even when they make a wrong turn looking for the bathroom and end up in the wine cellar. I marvel at their commitment to family and how loving five women can be all living under the same roof and often together around the clock. They enjoy each other's company and it shows. A party at their home is a true and honest representation of all things Maritime – lots of food, music, plenty of hugs, laughs and tears, pictures from yesteryear always on display and honest friendship even if months or years have passed since your last visit. You never have to explain why you have not been in touch.

Tucked away in my mother's black book are two pages written in her own handwriting. I am not sure if they are part of poems or published work but I love the simplicity of these words and they sound like my beautiful mother. On the first page appears, "Life is a journey – complete it … Life is a struggle – fight it." And on the second page is written –

> The six most important words are, "I admit I made a mistake."
> The five most important words are, "You did a good job."
> The four most important words are, "What is your opinion?"
> The three most important words are, "If you please."
> The two most important words are, "Thank you."
> The least important word is, "I."

Mom and I shared many things, much more than our cancer connection. She was my friend and we did many things together including attending concerts. There was a time in this fair land, during the 1980s, when my mother and I went, each year without fail, to a Gordon Lightfoot concert at Massey Hall in Toronto. Mom absolutely loved his music and looked forward to his concert every year. That is, until the year that Mr. Lightfoot introduced his new and much younger wife to the audience. Mom decided, on the spot, that she would not be attending another one of his concerts. I knew when she said it that she was serious – our annual outing to this particular gentleman's concert would happen no more. In the years that followed I did not attend concerts without her – it didn't seem right.

Fast forward to Sunday, May 13, 2007, at the Halifax Metro Centre and I, once again, attended a Gordon Lightfoot concert. My sister Connie, Carol Alexander and I made an evening of it and I couldn't help thinking that Mom just might be okay with me attending his concert after so much time had passed, and after all that he had been through.

When he took the stage he apologized for being a little late. In the fall of 2002, with a concert booked for Halifax, the legendary singer-songwriter suffered a serious abdominal haemorrhage and concerts were put on hold for some time. The apology was not necessary, but the crowd loved it.

At sixty-eight years of age he certainly could be forgiven for any cracks in his distinctive voice. Decades and decades into his hugely successful career he still draws an audience and he knows how to entertain. His songs flowed –"Cotton Jenny," "Sundown," "Ribbon of Darkness," "The Wreck of the Edmund Fitzgerald," "If You Could Read My Mind," "Baby Step Back," "Early Mornin' Rain" and so much more. I could picture Mom sitting beside me with that radiant smile on her face.

I have not had the opportunity to meet Gordon Lightfoot, although I almost did once. We both attended the *Maclean's* one hundredth anniversary gala. He was in the front row and I was in the back. I could see him but just couldn't get to him. Another time perhaps and I could tell him what his music meant to my mother – and to me.

As if my family has not seen its share of cancer, in 2008 my cousin Anna Taylor was diagnosed with B-cell lymphoma. A very ugly cancer had taken over half of Anna's face – literally. Anna is a fighter and she waged one hell of a fight with this disease, taking it one day at a time with her husband Ed by her side. Kathleen, Anna's daughter, and her son-in-law, Ghislain, came home following her initial diagnosis to be by her side and to make arrangements that Anna wanted taken care of "right now." That's our Anna. There would be more trips home.

Waiting for treatment is one of the most frustrating things a cancer survivor can go through and in my opinion Anna was forced to wait an unforgivable length of time before her chemo began. I hear this complaint from so many cancer patients who have to wait and wait for what is considered to be life-saving treatments to begin. It always seems so cruel. Immediately following her first chemo treatment – immediately meaning the next day – you could see an improvement in Anna's face. Part of her eye was now visible, the tumour was not as angry-looking and there was a small improvement in the swelling of her upper lip. The day after Anna's second chemo treatment even greater improvement could be seen. She was starting to look like our Anna again. A miracle.

A few weeks prior to Christmas 2008 Kathleen wrote to share her excitement about coming home from Ottawa to be with her mother for the holidays. "I am packing for our trip home to Saulnierville. We are going to spoil Mom rotten. I already mailed a five cubic box full of Christmas gifts for her. I bought her a nice new winter jacket, hats and mitts, a new housecoat and slippers and a whole lot of other things. My neighbour is sewing five new head scarves for me to bring to Mom. Ghislain wanted to buy something special for Mom that was just from him. He chose to buy her a beautiful diamond and gold chain called 'The Journey Collection.' This gift will acknowledge the journey she is going through. I am sure that she will cry when she opens it and understands the meaning behind it. This year it's all about my mom. She deserves it after everything that she has been going through and everything that she still has to go through. I can't wait to give her a big hug."

Anna and Kathleen are equally proud of each other. Like my son and me, they pretty much grew up together.

The evening before Anna's third chemo treatment in December 2008 we had dinner with her and her family at Swiss Chalet in Halifax, which was Mom's favourite restaurant too. The change in her appearance was almost impossible to believe. She looked wonderful. As Anna always does, she made fudge for us and she was her usual happy self – no self-pity for Anna.

We will walk on Mavillette beach in Nova Scotia with Anna and Ed for many years to come – I know it. I am so proud of how Anna has met this challenge. She has worked so hard to win. Her journey is not over but she is well on her way with her head held high.

Aunt Ann proudly wearing her Cornwallis Inn waitress uniform and posing with Uncle Andy's motorcycle.

Antoinette d'Entremont was my godmother and she took her role very seriously. In my eyes Aunt Ann, my mother's sister, led a very glamorous life. She worked at the Cornwallis Inn in Kentville and would share wonderful stories about her life there. Aunt Ann met many famous people staying at the inn and as a young girl it seemed to me she travelled extensively. She cared about her family and never forgot any of us. She met and married the love of her life, Paul Gregotski. Born February 13, 1917, in Meteghan River, Nova Scotia, Aunt Ann loved to tell stories about her family and those she met during her life's journey.

While growing up I loved the way Aunt Ann would seek me out for a few private moments when she visited our Wilmot home. We spoke about what she would like to do for me as my godmother. She

One of my most favourite pictures is of Mom, on the right, and Aunt Ann hugging each other. They look so happy and pleased with themselves.

reminded me that while I found her brother, my Uncle Andy, to be very exciting and wild I should remember that his lifestyle would never be for me. Years later when I attended my first Bell training course it happened to be in Hamilton where she and Paul lived. Andy lived there too. Sure enough, I hung out in bars (underage at the time) with Uncle Andy, who reminded me at evening's end to "not breathe a word to Ann." Wild and exciting indeed.

Two of the many things Aunt Ann gave me were her autograph books. They are very old and I cherish them to this day. One is dated October 22, 1931, and the other December 3, 1936. They contain funny quirky quotes like, "If you would enjoy your heavenly joys – think more of The Lord and less of the boys." My favourite is written by my mother and is dated December 6, 1936 –

> Dear Sister
> There isn't much use to say
> What you surely must have guessed
> That in all the world of folks today
> You are the one I love the best

The quote is signed M.R. d'Entremont and at the bottom of the blue page Mom's humour shines through with her added note, "May you never feel the color of this page."

When Mom and I were diagnosed with cancer Aunt Ann and I became closer – cancer does that to you, or for you. Because of this I had the opportunity to speak with Uncle Paul more often when I called their home or went to Hamilton to visit.

After Aunt Ann passed away Uncle Paul gave me her little black book, which not only contains details of her family and friends' births and subsequent deaths, it also records visits over the years and other things she felt were worthy of remembering. Dates from World War II share the same pages as the May 31, 1985, story of a tornado hitting Barrie, Ontario, and the October 17, 1989, date (5:04 p.m.) when San Francisco felt the big earthquake. She noted the date of her last visit to my condo in Toronto where she visited Mom on December 9, 1992 – Mom died later that month. I love the fact that Aunt Ann recorded so many things – Mom did the same thing and so do I.

I too am a godmother. Natalie Rose Mayne is my godchild and over the years we have found ways to maintain a special connection. Life gets in the way sometimes and when it does we don't feel guilty about it. We simply reconnect when we can. After my cancer recurrence in 2008 Lois, Natalie's mother, came to be with me for a month and she brought with her a lovely letter from Natalie.

Natalie is over forty now and she too has memories to share. And some relate to autograph books similar to the one my Aunt Ann kept so many years earlier. I wish I could say that I wrote something very profound in her first autograph book but that is not the case, although for some time, as a very young girl Natalie saw this as a cryptic message and somehow very much a secret message between the two of us –

> 2 Y's U R
> 2 Y's U B
> I C U R
> 2 Y's 4 Me

In addition to reminding me about her autograph book, Natalie's letter also points out the small things we can do to create memories for those we love. In a two-page letter she shared how she saw me when she was a child and how that view changed as she grew and became a mother herself. She admitted that she had a twenty-year infatuation with Rod Stewart after listening to my LPs and how she marvelled at my high-rise condo lifestyle.

After my cancer experience she saw me differently: "A few simple things about you have impacted me greatly. The joy I had in the simplicity of watching you in a thumb war with my two small children. The empowerment I received while listening to your experiences during one of your talks. The connection you share with my mother as you are both grandmothers and the adventure that brings. The courage, determination and strength with which you have battled cancer and in your development and success of the Comfort Heart Initiative will remain with me forever.

"I have always sensed you were a strong woman and in recent years I have watched the strength my mother has always had that I did not know was there. I believe all of the Cole sisters have exhibited great strength at times, though in their own way. I have seen the diverse creativity all of you possess. Perhaps, as I am in my own growth state right now, that is why I feel it is so important to acknowledge the impact you have made on me. I have truly realized the special gift I was given when you became my godmother. At various stages along our life path you have touched my soul and that is a gift that cannot be purchased and wrapped."

I love the memories that old pictures keep alive, and the images they help to create. July 4, 2007, I received a wonderful letter from a woman I had not met. Joan LeBlanc from Meteghan River read my books and wrote to thank me for the memories they brought back for her. Joan worked for Mumford's Drugstore in Middleton and she often visited with Mom during the early 1950s. She took the time to write a two-page letter filled with wonderful stories. She ended her letter by saying, "Excuse the mistakes in this letter as my education is very limited." I wrote back immediately to suggest that her life skills and experiences made her a PhD in my opinion and that I considered her letter a gift. Education comes in many forms and often the elderly need to be reminded just how educated they are. Joan included a picture of her aunt, Agnes Comeau, my Aunt Emelina and Mom (with her leg over Agnes's shoulder!). You can see the youth and confidence in the eyes of these teenage women.

Agnes Comeau, kneeling, Aunt Emelina on the left and Mom.

Miles Chipman and his family lived not far from our home in Wilmot. Miles and my father were friends of sorts and I earned my money during the summer picking strawberries on the Chipman farm. Milene was the oldest of the Chipman children and I saw her as the glamorous girl in our community. Everything about her seemed glamorous to me.

Milene and I reconnected in May 2003 when she attended an event in Alliston, Ontario, when I was the guest speaker. She e-mailed me shortly after. In part, she wrote, "I think perhaps the greatest achievement of your mother was to nurture the loving relationship she shared with her daughters in spite of the adversity. I often collected for the Red Cross, the Cancer Society and the Salvation Army and I always enjoyed my little chats with your mother when I knocked on your door. She had a knack of speaking to me as an equal … at least I felt more grown up in her presence. Also, she seemed to always have something good cooking so I don't know how you missed out on knowing how to cook!" I am sure that my mother did not have money to give to charity, so I was even more proud to hear of the positive memories Milene had of knocking on our door and spending a few minutes with Mom.

As a teenager it was apparent to me that my mother was willing to listen to my opinions. She taught me the importance of forming my own opinion after becoming informed about an issue. Mom and I often discussed the Steven Truscott case. The last time Lynne Harper was seen alive she was with Steven Truscott near the air base in Clinton, Ontario, where her father was an RCAF officer. It was June 9, 1959. Two days later they found her body and not long after that, on September 30, 1959, Truscott was convicted of capital murder. He was convicted by a jury and sentenced to death by hanging – the youngest person in Canada ever sentenced to death. Lynne Harper was twelve years old when she was murdered. Truscott was fourteen when he went to prison. He and I were almost the same age.

I first heard about the Truscott case when babysitting for friends of my father's at the Greenwood, Nova Scotia, airbase. The talk was fast and it sounded as if these people had been witness to the murder because they seemed to know it all. I remember being somewhat impressed that my father and his much younger air force pals knew this case in such detail that they could conclude in fact that Truscott was guilty and deserved to die. The next day I talked with Mom about what I had overheard. We were doing the breakfast dishes and we had a bit of alone time. Mom was quick to let me know that I should never assume others know everything or have all the facts. We talked about the difference between fact and fiction, the difference between knowledge and gossip. She asked me my opinion. I said then and I have always said that I thought Truscott was innocent. This case would remain of interest to me and it was one that Mom and I discussed whenever it was part of the news. Over the years it appeared to me that not all material had been before the courts in 1959. For some reason the legal experts saw what they wanted to see and ignored what they did not want to know; they needed the case to be closed.

Much has been written about possible suspects, including a sergeant at the nearby air force base with a disturbing psychiatric file, and who was previously charged for trying to lure a ten-year-old girl into his car. Following the murder, he suffered from anxiety, depression and guilt, according to an air force medical report in July of 1959. The Ontario Provincial Police never looked into the possibility that this man could be connected with the crime. He died in 1975. There was also an electrician with a rape conviction who worked at the air base and knew the family.

Probably because of the public anger over the planned execution of a child, Prime Minister John Diefenbaker and the federal cabinet commuted the sentence to life imprisonment in 1960. Cabinet minutes recorded Diefenbaker as saying, "The outcome would be reported all over the world and would undoubtedly reflect badly on Canada." No one seemed to doubt the verdict and no one was upset that police had arrested a boy, with no call to his parents, and questioned him for some twenty-four hours. He was tried as an adult with a lawyer who had three months to prepare. Within a couple of weeks the judge sent the boy to the gallows. Truscott sat on death row for four months until his sentence was commuted to life in prison.

A journalist, Isabel LeBourdais, published a book in 1966 called *The Trial of Steven Truscott* and it raised questions about his case. I did not read the book but heard of it via the media and Mom and I discussed it when I was home on vacation. It was a common thread in our library of topics to update for each other. I felt very adult-like when we talked about the Truscott case.

Paroled in 1969 after a decade behind bars, Truscott lived under an assumed name until 2000. He worked as a mechanical millwright and was known as Mr. Bowers. He and his wife Marlene raised three children.

The last discussion my mom and I had about this case was during the final months of her life in 1992. We were speaking about her diaries and some of the things she had written in them. I too had journalled this story and assured my mother that I would keep following the news and would keep her informed even when she was unable to journal any longer. We had a number of discussions about how Lynne Harper's family must have felt at the time of her murder and every day since then. If in fact Truscott was innocent, where was the murderer and would her family ever have closure? We had questions but no answers. I had a chance to thank Mom for discussing this with me so many years ago when as a thirteen-year-old I had been confused about the adult banter I had overheard. Mom rarely dismissed anything I wanted to talk about.

In 1997 Truscott met with lawyer James Lockyer and asked for his help in clearing his name. The wheels were put in motion. In

2000 Truscott went before the cameras and said he wanted to clear his name and would do everything possible to do that. He had the support of the Association in Defence of the Wrongfully Convicted. On August 28, 2007, the Ontario Court of Appeal acquitted Truscott, calling his murder conviction a miscarriage of justice. I thought about my mother. Truscott and his family received $6.5 million in compensation on July 7, 2008. He would say repeatedly it was not, and had never been, about money.

I will always relate the Truscott story to a bond I had with my mother – a bond where we shared life's struggles and stories covered in the media as well as what was happening in our own lives. My interest in "all things news" comes from my mother.

My mother worried that because her marriage failed this might have been the reason mine failed as well. Of course this was not the case. I am sure she was not the only mother who tried to take on the blame when something veered off the rails in her child's life. My mother gave me tons of advice when I was dating as a teenager but never did she advise me during my rocky marriage.

Advice often came from others, though. I received a letter from a man living happily in a small rural town in Manitoba after he read my second book. What stuck with me long after filing his letter away was one comment he had made: "I bet you will find your man by the time you write your next book and then you won't have to write about how great it is to be alone because you won't be alone anymore." News flash, buddy – we are often alone even when we are in a relationship.

There is very little that I envy about my married friends other than the history they have. I believe history helps a relationship when you are working through the tough days. Even if the history is less than positive the couple can look back and say, "We have weathered this storm before and we can do it again." If I married tomorrow I would have to hurry my history so I could enjoy it later in life.

Many married couples have a wonderful partnership and are truly happy. Many are not and some go so far as to say they envy the single lifestyle their friends seem to enjoy. When I hear this I am quick to remind them that *Sex and the City* is not reality. Single women and men are often at home on a Friday night just as they are. One is not better than the other.

The amount of money spent getting to and through divorce court is a disgrace. So much hard-earned money given to a legal expert who tells you what you often already know. It seems that each year couples are paying more and more for their divorce. If it is their divorce surely it should not cost every cent they have. To be fair to the lawyers, I realize that some people would prefer to give their hard-earned money to a lawyer rather than to the partner they are divorcing. It can be a mess.

Not to suggest I am a divorce expert. Although, having been divorced for more than thirty-eight years, I do have considerable experience responding to the "You're still not married?" question. I continue to jokingly answer the question by saying I don't want to rush into marriage again so am taking my time.

Divorce is not something we boast about or take pride in. It left a bitter taste in my mouth all those years ago. I had failed at something I believed in and it took considerable time for me to forgive myself. Over time I could admit that divorce takes courage and strength. It takes tons of honesty on both sides. It's not a case of saying, "I failed" but rather, "We failed" and the time comes to admit failure and move on in a positive way. Like the song says, "It takes two, baby, it takes two."

A woman I know says openly today that she was a little desperate when she hit the big five-oh and was still not remarried. She wanted to be married at that stage of life and in retrospect she feels she settled for someone she knew in her heart that she was really not compatible with. There was chemistry but it was faint. She married after a brief courtship, but at least she married before her fifty-first birthday, which was a major priority for her then. Now divorced for the second time she is in love with her online soulmate. I hope it works. The whole online dating thing doesn't ring true for me, yet I do have many friends who swear by it. I am convinced that it really does work – for them.

The term Happy Holidays can be a bit of an oxymoron for those divorced, widowed, and single and, yes, for married couples too who aren't all that happy. When friends say, "Are you going to be alone for the holidays again this year?" I am sometimes tempted to say, "Yes, you too?" even though I know they are married. Some of my most alone days have been when I was in the dying days of a relationship.

Happiness does not only come to couples. I understand there are more applications for divorce in January than in any other month of the year, proof that the Happy Holiday season is not always so happy.

Mom loved having dinner at the Old Mill restaurant in Toronto and as often as possible we shared Christmas dinner there. On one of our last holiday dinners at the Old Mill we were unfortunate to be sitting so close to a couple that we had no choice but to hear much of their holiday battle playing out as they badgered each other and vowed that they would be divorced before another Christmas approached. We were thankful to be leaving with each other.

After cancer and with maturity I am even more comfortable with my singleness. I wish I could share being-single stories with my mother today, especially some of the more humorous ones.

There are many other women from my mother's generation who did so much to create a better life for their children. My friend Dorothy's mother, Pearl Dunbar, lived in her three-bedroom home in Porcupine, Ontario, with her husband and six children. No running water and no indoor plumbing until Dorothy was sixteen. Her father was a miner from Truro, Nova Scotia, who died at the age of forty-four of lung disease caused by silicosis.

Our mothers went to work at about the same age and Mrs. Dunbar ran the service station that her husband had once operated. She did what she had to do for her kids. The gas pumps were in the front yard so she could work at the pumps and inside the home at the same time. She did it all as so many women have done, and continue to do.

Dorothy finished school and took a job at Hallnor Mines, part of the Noranda Mine. She soon realized she needed a change. With three of her friends by her side Dorothy made a well-researched decision to move to Kitchener, Ontario, to seek employment. After all, Kitchener had a great hockey team and this would be a great way to meet guys. The Unemployment Insurance office sent her to Bell Canada as it seemed Bell was looking for someone with her qualifications. Dorothy was given the job on the spot but turned it down because the pay was less than she had been making. She left the interview only to be called the following Monday morning saying she was late for work – they had found the money but neglected to inform her.

I met Dorothy on the job in 1978 when I was transferred from Ottawa to Toronto the first time. We worked well together, and even carved out gym time together at 6 a.m. near the office (of course). By the time she retired in 1993 Dorothy had worked in many different jobs and relocated many times. She called Kitchener, Oshawa, Thunder Bay, Sault Ste. Marie, Ottawa, Montreal, Kingston, Toronto, back to Thunder Bay and finally back to Toronto – home.

Dorothy thanks her mother for instilling in her a good work ethic. "Do not expect things handed to you on a silver platter. It is no disgrace to be poor. You simply work hard without complaint. If you can't change something you get over it and move on."

Dorothy and I are good friends to this day. In a way, our mothers introduced us.

I can't write about my mother without writing about Daisy Irene White (Murphy). The Whites and the Coles were neighbours in Wilmot, Nova Scotia, for many years. The White children are George, Phyllis, Dorothy, Jeannie and Karen. Phyllis and I were and are best friends. We recall often how our mothers would be standing either in their porch or ours waiting for the kids to arrive home from school. We don't remember our mothers visiting inside the home, only in the porch as if they were always at the ready to leave as soon their children appeared.

What we did not know as kids was that breast cancer would claim both of our mothers – Daisy far too soon. Daisy was born in 1924 and cancer killed her in 1979. She was in her early fifties when she first battled breast cancer. Often when Daisy had medical appointments her husband, George, would bring her to Halifax early so she could visit with Mom before going to see her doctor. When Phyllis was expecting each of her children her mother was battling cancer. Living in Montreal it was not easy for Phyllis to go home to be with her. When Chrissie was born, Daisy was battling a recurrence and literally stopped taking chemo so she could go to Montreal and hold her granddaughter. Phyllis has wonderful memories of how she and her mother laughed and cried together during that last visit. It was a gift her mother gave her. Daisy died shortly after that trip.

Mom, on the right, on her last day on the job at the Halifax Infirmary, June 30, 1981.

Christmas at the Halifax Infirmary, 1976.

Perhaps one day Holly, Phyllis's granddaughter, will become friends with my grandson Jalen and the connection between our two families will remain intact.

My mother had a huge collection of photo albums filled cover to cover with pictures of those she held dear – her family. On a good day just a few months prior to Mom's death we spent an entire Sunday afternoon going through her albums page by page, picture by picture. The photo she was most proud of was taken on her last day of work. Mom began working outside of the home at fifty and retired June 30, 1981, with a pension. She was a very strong and determined woman who taught her daughters what it means to hold your children forever close to your heart. It was not easy for her to work as hard as she did, but there was no question that she would do what she had to do in particular for her two young daughters who were still in school and looking to her for guidance and food on the table.

Mom took the time to tell me about one more picture. She had it pasted in her album with a note in her handwriting on the photo, "C.S.D Christmas 1976." I don't know the names of everyone in the photo with Mom but she spoke of how kind these women were to her and how they reached out to help each other as best they could. Parties like this were about more than exchanging gifts and sharing food. They were about finding the time to share positive thoughts and attending even if you were bone tired because you didn't want to let the others down.

Never a day goes by that I don't think about my mother. The more I learn about myself, the more I learn about her.

Simply Nancy

I have a few friends who have tried to gain weight. I have even more friends who have tried time and time again to lose weight. They don't have a personal trainer or a personal chef. Sometimes they reach their ultimate goal while other times they are not successful at all. Gaining and losing weight comes with a different set of issues for cancer survivors, especially those who have taken chemo. It is very often more difficult to lose the weight that for a variety of reasons sometimes comes with chemo and it ends up being an ongoing battle long after the cancer is gone. Nancy Stoddart has shared more of her weight-loss struggles with me than anyone else, and given that she finds success and does it with humour I have picked her story to share with you. She has not had cancer but I have often shared her e-mails about her weight issues with cancer survivors because of the way she tells her story. They can relate. Nancy concentrates on the health-related reasons to lose weight. I have learned so much from listening to her talk about her 2008 weight-loss agenda. Nancy types it like she says it (and she won a typing contest in high school so she types very fast).

About the weight loss and gain – yup – I'd likely be a good one to make comments. I've lost about sixteen tonnes in my lifetime. I lose it and I gain it. I lose it and I gain it again.

I've pretty much tried every diet and joined most every weight loss group around. I've been on South Beach and yes, I lost weight but no, I couldn't follow the diet for the rest of my life. Likewise with the soup diet, the carbohydrate/gram diet, the banana diet. I'm sure there are others if I just sat down and thought about it.

I was a TOPS (Take Off Pounds Sensibly) member. They don't give you a particular diet to follow. They weigh you every week so you do whatever you can to lose weight – sometimes not eating for a whole day before "weigh day"! I joined Weight Watchers but they didn't have the point system when I joined so members were on their own for a plan to lose. Now Weight Watchers has a point system and each food item is so many points. You're allowed to have a certain number of points a day. I could never follow a plan like that because I wouldn't write down or keep track of how many points I ate. I'd be looking for real food rather than points.

I tried hypnosis three times and it worked twice. Once the hypnosis wears off and the amount of food increases, the weight goes back on. As my health deteriorated and my arthritis got worse because I couldn't move around enough or walk enough to benefit my system, I decided that I had to do something that would be a lifetime change.

I joined Simply For Life. I have some friends who have been quite successful using SFL and have kept the weight off so, as a last resort, I thought I'd give it a try too. I decided in January 2008 that I really needed to do something. It was the end of March before I joined. I guess I thought if I put it off that it would go away. I had the right mindset when I joined and I also had determination and faith that if I was seeking professional help they would be able to steer me in the right direction. After working with a registered dietician for three and a half months I was thrilled to see that I had lost thirty-six pounds.

I don't feel like I'm on a diet. I'm eating very well and my energy level has improved immensely. I walk at least one kilometre every day in addition to the normal walking a person does in a day doing errands, etc. If I decide I want to have a chocolate (my favourite) or another treat I make sure I walk a little extra to burn it off. I haven't given up any particular food. I only eat butter when I have lobster but those two go together with me. As long as it's occasional, it's fine. I eat out at restaurants but make wise choices. Sometimes it's difficult because restaurants tend to add fat and salt to make their food taste better, and it does. I have found that it doesn't hurt to ask the waiter to check with the chef and ask him not to add extra salt or not to bread the fish but just grill it. Most are really good with special orders.

Excess weight magnifies other diseases. I work one-on-one with the dietician and she has some great tips, like don't eat carbs after lunch. Back in the 'olden days' we always had our big meal at lunchtime and our light meal at suppertime. That just makes perfect sense but in the modern world, people don't have time to eat dinner at noon so we have the light meal and then the heavy meal at suppertime and go to bed. I didn't set big goals at first but I can now change the goals if I wish and I likely will. I will continue to see the dietician after I go on maintenance and I'm sure her tips will help me very much. I have lots of support and no clothes.

I know for a fact that Nancy does have clothes. She also has a favourite clothing store – Frenchy's. If you are from the Maritimes you probably know the Frenchy's stores well. Shopping at Frenchy's is a social subculture that I was not familiar with until I moved home in 1996. I knew it was there but had not explored the actual stores. Used clothing is brought in every hour (according to Nancy) and if you time your visit correctly you can arrive for the next "dump" of clothing. I have been with Nancy on more than one of these shopping excursions and if you happen to arrive five minutes after the dump you must stay for at least another fifty-five minutes for the next. It works for her – she is always well-dressed and stylish when she needs to be. Saying, "I bought this top at Frenchy's for three dollars" is as good as holding up a trophy. The parking lot is often full of experienced shoppers who are back looking for their favourite designer. Count me in.

Just over six months after Nancy first adopted the SFL way of life we talked about her success and how SFL really isn't a diet at all. It is a way of life and it works. Nancy's weight loss reached sixty-five pounds and counting. She talked about a visit with her daughter and family in the U.S. and her goal during those two weeks to maintain her weight. She returned home minus one more pound and was thrilled. Often a vacation brings added pounds.

Nancy attended a seminar hosted by Bruce Sweeney, founder of Simply For Life, and was singing his praises. He spoke with passion to the audience and offered to help some individuals who needed and wanted to change their lives. Nancy was very impressed with his sincerity and is a strong supporter of this particular way to look at weight-loss options.

I took at look at the SFL website (www.simplyforlife.com) and decided it was worth sharing. Bruce and his team believe in doing one thing very well – helping people achieve their ultimate health through food. No pills, gimmicks or magic powers, just food from the grocery store.

In fairness, I have many friends who have met and maintained their personal weight goals with Weight Watchers, Take Off Pounds Sensibly and other organizations. It is an individual choice. In this case Nancy has chosen SFL and it has proven to be a good choice for her.

The last time I asked Nancy about her total weight loss she was proud to say, "Down seventy-five pounds and counting."

Pauline Baxter Moore and Her $800,000 Gift

*F*or many years I have known the name Pauline Baxter Moore. I have always known there was a powerful story behind her name but did not fully understand the details of her story. That changed in December 2007 when I attended the Bell Canada Scarborough Retiree Club Christmas luncheon with Jeanette Fitzgerald. I left the luncheon with the desire to learn all I could about Pauline Baxter Moore, this angel to so many.

Jeanette had lost her beloved Jack to cancer on March 22, 2007, and was attending her first Scarborough Christmas party alone. Actually, even though I was with her I know she felt alone without her Jack. That type of aloneness must be enormous – I can't even imagine. Jeanette later shared with me that her mind kept going back to previous luncheons with Jack at her side and each time someone asked how she was doing it added to her sadness. I was so proud of her as I observed people approaching, a number of whom had not seen her since Jack's death. Many did not know what to say and she handled it all so well. She listened, she commented and even managed a smile or two. Each person finished their conversation and left feeling better. Jeanette was able to give others a Christmas gift of a smile and a memory of Jack.

As we enjoyed lunch and renewed friendships I heard Pauline Baxter Moore's name mentioned again and again. Years after her retirement from Bell and years after her death we continued to speak about her. The gift she left to so many was huge — absolutely huge. And it's quite a story.

Born in Cornwall, Ontario, in 1912, Pauline moved to the U.S.A. and began her career with Pennsylvania Bell in 1929. In 1942, after the United States entered World War II, Pauline moved back to Canada and transferred to what was then called the Bell Telephone Company of Canada.

I had the pleasure of confirming much of this information, and learning even more from Marjorie Henderson, a personal friend of Pauline's. I had an appointed time to call Marjorie and she was clearly ready for my call. For some fifty minutes she shared her memories about her friend. She even read a speech about Pauline that she was developing to give at a luncheon. Marjorie speaks so fondly and proudly of Pauline and enjoys sharing her knowledge about Pauline with others. They travelled to work together and became lifelong friends. Their daily conversations strengthened their friendship.

As the summer of 1967 approached, that particular timeline saw me preparing for marriage, and Pauline preparing for her retirement. She had been very active in volunteer work during her career and as a pensioner she continued to give back. She was a Pioneer Life Member and regularly attended meetings of the Fieldway Life Member Club where she enjoyed many hours of friendship and companionship. Pauline took considerable pride in her career and in the company for which she had worked.

In 1985, two years before her death, she wrote her will, leaving her entire estate of some $800,000 to be used for fellowship at these Bell functions. She explained that having had so much pleasure from attending these meetings/celebrations she wanted to ensure that others would continue to enjoy what she had enjoyed for so many years. While a substantial amount was spent on legal advice to ensure that Pauline's money continues to be used as she wished, the remaining funds are certainly put to good use.

In addition to covering legal fees associated with managing Pauline's gift, her money is used to pay rent for the Telco Community Volunteer Retiree Club meetings. It subsidizes club luncheons and Christmas parties, as well as the much-enjoyed bus trips to see a play or visit Niagara on the Lake. These are trips that many Bell pensioners would otherwise not be able to make. Pauline's legacy will be alive long after the money is gone. That's how it should be.

This story is not about the ugly side of the reality we sometimes see when money is involved. It is the inspirational story of one woman who found a way to give back long after her death.

And it is about Jeanette Fitzgerald and all of the other women and men who have lost their partners and boldly carve their own path in this world, leaving two footprints where there once would have been four.

Stories like these inspire me.

Shauna Marie MacLean and Her Red Shoes

I met Shauna Marie MacLean from New Waterford, Nova Scotia, while attending the World Conference on Breast Cancer. Shauna is young to have already experienced the ravages of breast cancer. In 2008 she became the poster woman for a fundraising campaign and when we met she was preparing for a radio commercial, a television commercial, a storefront window display and a mailer that would go out to over sixty thousand homes in Cape Breton. Shauna calls it "finding the silver lining in my cloud." She is wise beyond her years and I am proud to share her story, in her own words.

Life was going along pretty smoothly until October 22, 2006. That was the day I found a lump in my right breast while showering. As soon as I felt that lump I instantly felt panic ... as though something was telling me this was huge. Through my tears I yelled for my husband and when he came into the bathroom I told him what I had found. I asked him to feel the lump to see if it was really there. It was. He immediately told me not to worry because he didn't think it was anything serious. I spent the rest of the day worried and stressed. I decided that evening that I would go to see Dr. Azer before heading to work in the morning. I didn't sleep very much that night. I was a basket case. I was thirty-eight years old.

I went to Dr. Azer's office at 9 a.m. on October 23 and when his secretary saw me she knew something was wrong. I never just pop in to the office. When she asked how she could help me I instantly started to cry

... *having to say I had a lump in my breast to someone else just made it that much more real. I asked when I would be able to see the doctor and she told me to sit down and wait because he would see me as soon as he came in for the day. I took a seat and then called work to let them know I would be late.*

I saw Dr. Azer about ten minutes later and as I tried to explain to him why I was there I immediately started to cry ... reality really can bite. He asked me not to tell him where the lump was located so he could see if he could find it on his own. The lump was large so it was easy to find. He explained to me that he thought it was a fibrous mass but that because of my age he would send me for a mammogram to just make sure.

Before I left, Dr. Azer's secretary, Trish, told me that she would be contacting me by the end of the day to let me know when I would be having my mammogram. She was true to her word because by lunchtime she had already called me back to let me know that my mammogram would be November 6.

I had my mammogram and the results came back negative. I then had an ultrasound a couple of weeks later — another negative test result. A few weeks after that I had a core needle biopsy. Once again a negative test result. For some reason I did not have confidence in any of these test results. I felt strongly there was something wrong with me. I discussed this fact with Dr. Azer and he referred me to a surgeon. I relaxed a bit at that point and just tried to get on with my life.

A new opportunity presented itself at work and I applied to switch accounts and be a customer service supervisor on the Bell Canada account. I attended a six-week training program which was on the night shift and I became very tired. I thought the fatigue and weight loss I was experiencing could be attributed to the late-night training, having a four-year-old, a husband and just getting over the fact that I had nearly lost my sister and nephew during her pregnancy. Life was busy.

I finally saw the surgeon — April 23, 2007 — much time had passed. Too much time in my opinion. Instantly I did not have a good feeling about the surgeon. She examined me and told me I have fibrocystic breasts from drinking too much coffee and just getting older in general. Keep in mind that I never drink more than one cup of coffee per day. I left the surgeon's office very frustrated and felt that I had been brushed off.

I saw the same surgeon a month later and that visit didn't go any better than the first one. She told me I was overreacting — it was nothing and that I should go home and live my life. At that point I became irate. I demanded that she remove the lump from my breast. She tried to deter me by saying I didn't want to have a scar on my breast because it would make mammograms that much harder to read in the future. I nearly lost my mind at this statement and demanded once again that she remove the lump. She conceded and scheduled me for my surgery for June.

On June 29, I had my lumpectomy. It was a circus from the very moment I entered the hospital. I was scheduled to have a wire inserted into my breast and the lump would be removed that way. When I got to the ultrasound department to have the wire inserted I noticed that the technician was setting up on the wrong side. I asked the tech what she was doing and she said she was going to do an ultrasound on my left breast … problem is the lump was in the right breast. Not a great way to start the day. Needless to say, there was a bit of an uproar at that discovery. Within minutes there was another technician and two radiologists in the room; a huge discussion took place where they tried to convince me that they were doing my left breast. Finally, someone made a call to the surgeon's office and much to their chagrin I was right after all. Then came the profuse apologies. I let them know that it was not their fault; they could only go by the information they had been given on the paperwork and it had been filled out incorrectly.

After all of this, the wire procedure was cancelled and a regular ultrasound was performed, my breast was marked and back up to day surgery we went. A short while later it was time to head to the operating room and the lumpectomy was performed.

When I woke up in the Recovery Room I remember the nurses saying everything had gone very well and shortly thereafter I was wheeled back to the day surgery waiting area. The surgeon came in to see my husband, Sheldon, and I to talk about how the surgery had gone and at that time she said, "If this is breast cancer, I'll find a new job." Naturally, we were relieved to hear that statement and to be quite honest with you I went home that day very confident that I did not have cancer.

I went back to work the following Monday and life had returned to normal once again. I didn't have cancer so I could stop worrying. Wrong.

On July 18 I picked up a voicemail at work and in that very instant my life forever changed. My family physician's secretary had left a message that I needed to be at my doctor's office at 3 p.m. that afternoon. He does not have office hours on Wednesday – that is his day to work at the can-

cer centre in Sydney. There was no need for her to say what was wrong. I knew in my gut and my gut never lies. I immediately called my husband, who happens to be a paramedic and was in the cancer centre with a patient at that time, to let him know about the phone call. He had to hang up for a couple of minutes and asked me to stay at my desk so he could call me back. He called me to let me know that he would be leaving work at noon so he could be with me at that appointment. I was crying and he was doing his best to keep me calm – almost an impossible task. After we hung up I went to talk to my manager to let him know that I would have to leave early to attend a doctor's appointment. When he asked if everything was okay I started to cry. He wished me luck and sent me home.

It was the longest afternoon of my life. The time seemed to drag on; each minute was like an hour. At around 2:30 p.m. Sheldon and I went for a short drive so we could try to collect our thoughts and then it was time to meet with Dr. Azer. As we walked in I could feel the tension in the air. Trish did not make eye contact and was not her usual chatty self. A couple of minutes later Dr. Azer came out to get us and as we sat down he said, "I don't have good news." I told him that I didn't think he did.

Dr. Azer explained what had been found: invasive and ductal lobular cancer. I would be having a modified radical mastectomy in nine days. At that statement I told him I would be having both breasts removed and he told me I would have to discuss that with the surgeon. As the topic of a surgeon was raised I told him that I was not comfortable with having the same surgeon do the mastectomy and he told me he would do his very best to try to get me another.

Dr. Azer spent over an hour with us and was an absolute godsend on that fateful day. Before we left the office I was made to say, "I have cancer." It was one of the most difficult things I've ever had to do but it was what I needed. Hearing those words come from me made it that much more real.

When we left the office we went to my in-laws to tell them. They were shocked. After that it was time to tell my mother – torture. To see the look of fear in her eyes hurt me so deeply. My sister was home that day so she heard it when Mom did. There were a lot of tears and even more questions. Unfortunately, our son, Adam, was at Mom's that day so he found out at that time that Mommy was sick. He asked some questions and I answered them the best way I knew how, with honesty. I told him that Mommy had a sick "boobie" and that the doctor was going to take it *off and throw it in the garbage ... simplistic, I know, but it worked for us. I didn't want to hide things from him but at the same time he did not need to know that cancer could possibly kill me.*

I then went in to work ... crazy, huh? I wanted to let them know what was going on and how things were going to proceed. Next I went to my best friend Rachael's house to tell her what we had just found out. We hugged, cried and just chatted for a while. It was time to head for home and try to get some rest because I knew I was in for a long week. I had been given a prescription for Ativan so I filled it and I used it that day. Believe it or not I actually slept that night. The next morning when I woke it was like I was in a bad dream. I had cancer. I had an abdominal ultrasound scheduled for that morning and I had decided that I would go alone because I was okay.

I had the ultrasound and when the technician said, "I'm just going to check on your pictures," I completely lost it. I was a bucket of tears and completely inconsolable. The poor girl didn't know what to do with me. My husband has a friend who is a nurse and she came down to try to get me back together. It took a little while but it worked. Now that was embarrassing. I'm sure that technician still cringes when she sees me.

There was lots to do to get ready for surgery including seeing my favourite surgeon. The appointment was the following Tuesday and once again it was a circus. The secretary had called to book the appointment but when we got there she asked why we were there. One more time we were stunned by the way we were being treated. This set the mood for the whole appointment. By the time we got to see the surgeon I was livid and it only got worse from there. When she came into the exam room she had a resident with her and she asked if she could come in the room with us. I said No, I didn't want anyone else in the room. This was hard enough to hear without strangers there to observe.

I was very angry and I completely let loose. I had a lot to say and most of it wasn't very nice. My husband, who normally says very little, had so much to say that I actually wondered if someone had kidnapped my real husband and sent a replacement. The discussion was heated at best and at one time the surgeon stated that if I had so little confidence in her then perhaps I should find another surgeon to do the procedure. I let her know that I had already tried but the person I wanted was on vacation and we were stuck with each other. Not surprisingly, this went over like a lead balloon. The next topic of discussion was that I wanted bilateral mas-

tectomies. Along came another explosion. The doctor explained that there would be a much higher risk of depression if I proceeded this way. Who cares? I can take a pill for that, can't I? She told me that in order to do bilateral surgeries she would have to cancel someone else and I told her to go ahead. She told me that if I contracted an infection it would delay my treatments and in return I asked if she could guarantee that I would not get an infection if she only did the right side. You know the answer to that question.

After a long and very heated conversation she conceded to the bilateral mastectomies. I was scheduled for July 27.

July 27 came very quickly. We got to the hospital and registered and went upstairs to the surgical waiting area. Sheldon was with me, of course, as were his parents, my mom, Sheldon's aunt and uncle from Oshawa, and his aunt Florence from Sydney. We took up the whole waiting area. I was scheduled for noon but they came to get me at 11:30. I wasn't ready. I hugged and kissed everyone, and Sheldon and I headed to the operating room holding area. The anesthesiologist came to see me. The surgeon came to see me and she once again tried to talk me out of bilateral surgeries. A few minutes later I walked into the operating room and all I remember thinking is "Holy crap it's cold in here." A nurse came over to get me ready to be put to sleep and then it was time to have a nerve block placed in my back to make the pain more manageable. As this was being done the surgeon, again, tried to talk me out of the bilateral; at that point I got rude and will not tell you what I said. She immediately backed off and proceeded to get ready for surgery. A few minutes later I was being put to sleep and the next time I opened my eyes I was in Recovery.

I was only in the hospital for three days and was very happy to be able to go home. I could not wait to sleep in my own bed and be with my family. The day I got home was bittersweet. I was happy to be there but my drains obviously scared my son, who asked if that was my blood in the drains and if all of my blood was going to fall out. That was hard.

The VON nurses came every day for three weeks to change my dressings and make sure everything was healing properly. There were some small setbacks with minor infections and sutures getting yucky but all in all healing went well. There were lots of gifts, meals and flowers. For some reason almost everything was pink. I always hated pink. Funny how I would end up with a disease that is signified by the colour I liked least.

It was difficult not being able to be alone with our son, not allowed to drive and not able to do much at all. And then there's the no shower thing. Talk about frustration — no matter how often I sponge bathed myself I still did not feel clean.

Finally it was time for my post-op checkup and yet another face-to-face with the surgeon. During this appointment she let me know that due to our personality conflict she would no longer treat me, but much to her surprise I already knew this because my family doctor had already given me a copy of her letter. I told her how I felt about her and that I thought it was a good idea for her not to treat me any longer. I made sure I was able to shower and drive and off I went.

In August I saw my medical oncologist, Dr. Hussein, for our first meeting. We discussed what my treatment regime would be and that it was subject to change when the final pathology came back. When I went for my first chemo on August 20 I found out that my drug had changed because there had been three lymph nodes involved. I would have three treatments of FEC5 and three treatments of Taxotere. Chemo itself was easy for me but the IV access was torture. I was scheduled to have a porta-cath inserted in my chest to make things easier. My portacath was inserted on August 28 and that procedure was a nightmare. The barbarian who did the procedure did not believe in freezing or sedation so I was aware of everything and felt the scalpel cut through my skin to access my jugular vein. Yep, you heard right.

Exactly two weeks after my first chemo my hair started to fall out in clumps and it was very painful. Hair is sharp at the root and when I would lie down it would hurt a great deal.

On September 2 I contacted a professional photographer in my area, John Ratchford, to see if he would be interested in documenting my journey through breast cancer. He jumped at the chance and four days later I had my first photos done; some were clothed and some were topless. John was the epitome of professionalism and did not make me self-conscious at all. Keep in mind that I would have never had topless photos taken before breast cancer. It's funny how breast cancer can change your outlook on things.

Those first pictures were liberating; I am still a woman, I am still me. Although I looked very tired in the first pictures, when I look at them now I am reminded of how far I have come, a very long way. In the beginning I did not know where I was headed nor did I know if I was going to survive this horrible beast we call breast cancer. I had some days where I didn't want to fight anymore but they were far outnumbered by the days where I fought like a lion to beat this illness.

When I was first diagnosed I received an e-mail from a co-worker who had recently fought brain cancer and won. She told me to remember one very important thing. Her motto throughout her fight was, "I have cancer. Cancer does not have me." Thank you, Kelly. Even now I still use this motto, which became my mantra during the hard times when I didn't think my body or my mind could take anymore punishment.

The first three chemo treatments were easy. I did not get physically sick and in fact I went back to work part-time after chemo number two. The next three were not so easy. It was Taxotere and that was followed by an injection of Neulasta twenty-four hours later. The injection causes your bone marrow to work overtime and it causes bone pain. I have never felt pain like that before and within forty-eight hours it was almost crippling for me. The extreme pain only lasted for a couple of days but it seemed like months. With each consecutive Neulasta treatment the pain came harder and faster. As a matter of fact, I ended up in the hospital overnight from dehydration and I needed four litres of fluids to get me back to where I needed to be. That was a scary day. Dehydration does weird things to your body: you can't think, you can't reason and you have no idea why. I was learning so much.

Chemo finished on December 12, 2007. Christmas was going to be almost normal – well, except for being bald. Keep in mind that I sported my bald head proudly. I did not wear a wig. I had one at home but to me it symbolized illness and being bald just made people think I was weird. You see, I never looked like I was sick.

On New Year's Eve we went to a dance with friends and had an amazing time. This evening had a whole new meaning for me because in July I did not know if I would see this night. There were lots of laughs, tears, and hugs. Midnight meant I had reached another milestone that I had set for myself: to be alive in 2008.

On January 2 I started radiation treatments and I went every day for twenty-five days. My skin was red and itchy by the end of week two and it was angry by the end of week three. Week four brought more pain and so did week five. I think I only missed a couple of days at work throughout this time period. It was easier than chemo but definitely more painful on a daily basis. I like to refer to those weeks as being popped in the microwave on high for three minutes a day. It was like the worst sunburn you have ever had multiplied by at least ten.

Radiation finished on February 5 and it was a bittersweet day. Treatment and the frequent appointments were over so what do I do now? I saw my oncologist on February 28 and he informed me that I was NED, No Evidence of Disease.

On my way home that day I bought myself a pair of red patent leather shoes. They have become my trademark – to celebrate being alive.

During this time my family doctor asked if I would be interested in getting involved with the Regional Hospital Foundation in order to help raise funds for the expansion and upgrades to our local Cancer Centre and I immediately jumped at the chance. My photos were used in a fundraising appeal that went out to sixty thousand homes in Cape Breton. I was invited to speak at a major dinner they have every year and I am called the face of the campaign. I have radio spots, a TV commercial and two radio interviews. I have chosen to take my story public and put myself out there to help raise money to expand and upgrade our Cancer Centre because having it here allowed me to have all of my treatments close to home. I never had to leave Cape Breton even one time for treatment and to me that was one of the most important factors in my recovery.

In June I was lucky enough to be one of the recipients of a full bursary to attend the Fifth World Conference on Breast Cancer in Winnipeg, Manitoba. It was an amazing few days, very emotional and uplifting. I met so many other women who had walked in my shoes and won. Some have survived for more than twenty years since their diagnosis. Some have battled the disease for many years, with recurrence and metastasis but still have the same fight-like-a-lion attitude that I have.

I took my pictures to the conference and shared them with many people. We all had so much in common; we spoke the same language. We all spoke in medical terms and actually understood each other. We are a huge club that no one wants to belong to – the breast cancer club.

Since finishing treatment and travelling to Winnipeg I have been able to speak to a few women who have been newly diagnosed, and I like to think I have helped them in their journey. I have received many e-mails and voicemails about what I have chosen to do with my breast cancer. I am helping other women in their fight to slay the dragon, and I am not done yet!

Shauna and I have kept in touch via e-mail since our first meeting and her Nova Scotia spirit comes through with each note she writes. She has made the decision to love her battle scars and not have reconstruction. She is okay with who she is and has learned to love her new body. I heard from her as she celebrated her eight-months-and-counting cancer free mark and she had already replaced her first pair of red shoes. "Wore 'em out!"

A plaster mold of her torso has been made for use as a teaching tool at Dalhousie University's School of Nursing. Completed by an art student at the Nova Scotia College of Art and Design University it was a very long process but Shauna tells me it was well worth it. Her torso-mold serves as a valuable resource for women who are about to go through a mastectomy. Shauna is well on her way to accomplishing her goal to help others deal with this dreaded disease.

John Ratchford, Shauna's photographer, says it has been a "humbling beautiful privilege to journey with Shauna this way." His work won Best Feature Album at the 2009 Professional Photographers of Canada Atlantic Print Competition. And he suspects the album, and Shauna, will go on and on.

We will see and hear much more about this remarkable woman.

Kelly Bergshoeff

Kelly Bergshoeff says that what she knows now is that after battling cancer at a very young age, and its physical and emotional challenges and after a career change that did not bring the satisfaction she thought it would, she remains positive with a goal to ensure her two daughters learn from her and see her as a positive influence in their lives. Her priorities are in check. Although this was not the case after she hit her one year of being cancer free.

Priorities were not in check, life was not working out the way she had hoped it would and her career had taken a drastic turn. Kelly struggled with all the emotional side effects of cancer, the ones nobody talks about when chemo and radiation are complete and your hair grows back and the cancer support groups are focused on the newly diagnosed and the survivors are left to pick up the pieces and move ahead.

Due to her drastic weight loss during chemo, the doctors insisted on putting Kelly on prednisone, which ultimately led to weight gain. With this weight gain came low self-esteem because of the loss of her breasts, and eventually depression. Two years after fighting the battle of her life, she realized that it really wasn't over. She had so many more struggles ahead of her. When all her family rallied around her, they convinced her that she should not let cancer define who she is. She needed to see the gift she was given, the gift of life, and how her history could change the path of the future for her children. Only then did Kelly set her own destiny.

Kelly joined a post-cancer support group that gave her the courage to move aside what was weighing her down and allowed her to focus on the positive, putting the negative in the past. Kelly realized that life had so much more to offer. She had the wonderful support of her husband and family, along with two beautiful girls who needed her in their lives.

Within a year she weaned herself off the anti-depressants and the steroids. This allowed her to focus on her goal of getting back in physical shape. Kelly started walking forty-five minutes per day, five days a week as her oncologist advised that being in good physical health would be a benefit in case of a recurrence of cancer.

Although Kelly made a career change after the cancer diagnosis which did not give her the expected results, she remains positive about all aspects of her life. She is now a mentor for newly diagnosed breast cancer women, runs in the CIBC Run for the Cure every year with her two daughters, and does the Survivor Lap every year at the Relay for Life.

Today, she considers herself a performer in her own show. She sets the stage, she determines the impact on her life and she determines how her positive actions have an impact on others.

Kelly lives life to the fullest, thanking God everyday for the gift He gave her.

The Good Neighbours' Club

Since I battled cancer again it has been good therapy for me to continue to volunteer outside of the cancer community. The Good Neighbours' Club has been part of my life for many years and I feel comfortable in this environment where so many could use a helping hand. These men don't know about my cancer history and their history is unknown to me. It's a good fit.

The Christmas parties for the club members have been occurring at Saint Paul's Basilica in Toronto for over twenty years. Bell pensioners, employees and friends mark the party date in their schedule early in the year because everyone wants to help and share in the celebration. The giving of this party is a gift to the members and a gift to all of us as well.

The Good Neighbours' Club is a day centre for the older, homeless and unemployed men in the Toronto area and is often called one of Toronto's best kept secrets. Founded in 1933 and with over five thousand names on the membership list, the GNC is a safe and warm facility for financially disadvantaged, unemployed or unemployable senior men in Toronto. On any given day you will see between 150 and two hundred men spending their day at the club. Doors are open from 7 a.m. to 7 p.m. seven days a week with minor exceptions during July and August. A registered charity, the GNC operates with a volunteer board of directors and a small professional staff. Core funding comes from the City of Toronto, Ministry of Health (Ontario government) and the United Way of Greater Toronto. Fundraising for the club is critical, and when so many organizations are looking for assistance it seems to become more difficult in the current economic environment to fundraise to meet goals. It is a worry.

Often at hostels, checkout time is 7 a.m. so GNC members are anxious to meet up with their friends and begin their day with coffee and a muffin. Staff at GNC work on a very personal level with the club members. They manage daily cash allowances for some, coordinate the use of shower and laundry facilities, monitor hygiene habits, provide clothing, mail service, telephone service and ensure the card/games room is always up and running. Many of the club members have struggled with depression, addiction, homelessness and mental health issues. The staff has been successful in helping many of these men to stabilize their lives, regain their health and find safety and peace.

Noon hour is the busiest time of the day. Between 11:30 and 12:30 the club offers a hot, hearty, nutritious full-course meal for which the members are asked to pay twenty-five cents if they can. Lunch is provided for some two hundred members each day and three times a week an evening meal is also served. I have witnessed the appreciative faces on the members as they silently line up for lunch. I find it very humbling to observe this and I respect their feelings when they want to be left alone.

The club relies heavily on volunteers. The volunteers, for example, visit the sick and shut-in members. They deliver mail, cheques, books, magazines and the most important of all – good cheer. If a member goes missing the volunteer team swings into action. At life's end, when a member dies, the club liaises with the right people to ensure a proper service and burial. The Christmas party is another example of the role volunteers play.

For members, the GNC is indeed the one place they can call home. They appreciate having their own membership card and they are grateful for all that the club gives to them. For the most part, they are very positive men. If I told you that one of the members changed his name to Happy Ness Charron you might guess that his life story is a totally positive one. Guess again.

Happy has written a number of books and he shares very openly that his life began in less than positive circumstances. His mother died hours after he was born. His alcoholic father neglected him and gave him beatings that no child should endure. Worst than that, his dad accused Happy of murdering his wife. For many years Happy believed this. By the tender age of thirteen he was an alcoholic and found himself in prison several times during his youth.

Theodore (Ted) Anthony Charron officially became Happy Ness Charron in 1963 and today he is a successful author, traveller, motivational speaker, much loved father, grandfather and friend to many. His books are worth checking out – *2000 Adventures of a Man Called Happyness*, *Finding Happy Ness* and *Buried Treasure*. Happy is a busy man who can often be found with his friends at the club.

I have seen Happy at the club and at the Christmas parties over the years but had not met him personally. That changed at the December 2008 party. I observed from the back of the room as he greeted fellow club members and staff. He went out of his way to thank the volunteers and he approached me with an outstretched hand and a smile that warmed my heart. Happy is seventy-four years young, happy and healthy. He was excited to tell me that he would be spending Christmas with his family. He is still writing, still travelling and still enjoying the life he has carved out for himself. In mid-2009 I followed up with Happy and he had more news. "In March of 2009 I changed my name again. I have been Bad Bobby, Terrible Ted, Happy Ness and now I am Happy Happy on my brand new birth certificate!" You can read more about Happy on his website www.happyness.ca.

Hard times can happen to anyone. During a Christmas party luncheon as I served sandwiches to one table in particular, a youthful-looking man noticed my Order of Canada pin and softly said, "Congrats to you on the award. My old man has one of those." I wanted so much to ask him more but the time was not right. I have seen him at subsequent Christmas parties and we exchange a private smile. He doesn't want to talk about it, and I try to imagine the details of his life's journey that have brought him to GNC for his Christmas meal.

In the beginning there was no Christmas music played at the annual party. The members did not want to be reminded of the season. We began with a band of two playing country and western music. Over the years the music grew to include Christmas songs (if requested by the members) and the band grew to eight or nine musicians from all backgrounds, professional and amateur. They rent the equipment needed to make the day a musical one and come from miles away to see the smiles on the faces in the audience.

We gather early on party day to put together the goody bags containing items the members can use daily: t-shirt, hat, gloves, scarf, toothbrush, toothpaste, socks, candy and dozens and dozens of other things, all donated. This is a great improvement from the days when we would collect slightly used socks rather than the new ones now donated. When we first began the parties, a pack of cigarettes was the most appreciated gift in the goody bag and over the years we began cutting back to only a few cigarettes. The word spread very quickly the year we did not give cigarettes at all. The first few men to receive their gift checked quickly for "a smoke" and wasted no time in letting the others know that we had taken their cigarettes away totally. It was the right thing to do but often the right thing to do is not appreciated and this was certainly the case. They got over it and they understand. Sadly, many of them still smoke. You can see them leaving the party every fifteen minutes or so to have a smoke outside. I hope it doesn't kill them. History would suggest it will in many cases. It is heartbreaking.

As a two-time cancer survivor I find it impossible to not continually speak out about the fact that smoking kills. I am not alone. Dawn, a woman I have never met, e-mailed me on March 20, 2009, to share her view. "I am a come-from-away, originally from England. I moved to Cape Breton in 2001. I was recently at my mother's side as she passed way from lung cancer. I find it hard to forgive her for inflicting this on us, her family and herself. She smoked from the age of fourteen. There are enough things out there to get us, [so] why open the door and invite them in." Her note took me back to the year we eliminated cigarettes from the GNC Christmas bags. I could not help but wonder how many of these men were victims of others who smoked around them in their early days.

On party day, coffee is ready when the first member comes through the door. They come early in their best clothes and in rain or shine. If the weather is good we could see over three hundred members. They love coffee and drink it constantly. Having enough coffee all the time is one of our greatest challenges at the party.

We don't serve the Christmas turkey with all of the trimmings. We serve many different types of sandwiches, plain cheddar cheese, cheezies, chips and pretzels. Crusts are cut off the sandwiches for a couple of reasons. Some of the men have dental issues and the sandwiches are easier to eat without the crust and secondly, and more important, it makes the men feel good because we have done something a little bit extra for them. We have come to know there are sandwiches they don't like and we know they particularly love the rolled-up peanut butter and banana sandwiches – I do too. And no fancy cheese please – brie goes untouched. And eggnog. Lots and lots of eggnog. Again, everything is donated.

We all fondly recall the year a club member, an artist, presented a small token of thanks to the chair of the party committee. He took one of the small sandwich plates and on the plain back of the plate he copied the mural in the basement of the church and wrote, "Thank you for your efforts."

Santa always comes to the party. At the end of the celebration the members line up to shake Santa's hand and receive their gift. They take care of their own and if a friend can't make it they ask for an extra gift bag to be delivered personally. We line up too and we are proud to shake every hand and offer a holiday greeting of our own. The men make eye contact when they say, "Thank you" and their handshake is often firm and personal – many shake with both hands. I love this part of the party.

Every man at the club has his own history and each individual history is different. Often their eyes say, "I had a life. A full life." For now, the club is their life. There are similar clubs everywhere and I suspect they could all use an additional volunteer, another pair of hands to help.

The economic issues in 2008 made it harder than ever for the GNC to continue to offer all the services that members have become familiar with and take advantage of on a daily basis. Rising costs to maintain the building, repair worn-out equipment, purchase supplies and pay staff salaries added up to more money than was available and fundraising became more critical than ever before. These members should not suffer any more than they have already. In a world where company CEOs retire or take leave of their post with a multi-million-dollar payout it seems that belt-tightening is still forced on those who have nothing left to give. I hope and pray we will see the GNC alive and well for years to come with funders, volunteers and members working together.

When we give the gift of volunteering we often receive the greatest payment of all in the form of a heartfelt smile – sometimes a sad smile which speaks volumes. Like the other volunteers, I look forward to the Christmas party each year. At day's end I leave with the reminder that every face has a story behind it and I must never assume I know that story. Humbling indeed.

Writing a Memoir

*B*arbara Harvey is a hero of mine. Surviving cancer is not what makes her a hero. It's about how she plays the card that life has handed her. Barb and I first met in 1981 when I transferred into Bell's installation and repair district in Toronto and she was one of my assistants. At that time neither of us would have guessed the dreaded cancer would come looking for both of us.

On December 22 (my mom's birth date), 1997, Barb was diagnosed with ALL – Acute Lymphoblastic Leukemia. She was referred to the hospital for some tests and was admitted within hours. Barb was a very ill woman and chemo began dripping through her veins only two days later. She would not be home for Christmas. Not much to celebrate that holiday season. Barb's chemo did not finish until May of 2000, two and a half years later. She would be the first to admit there were times she worried that cancer would indeed kill her. I did too. Given a 40 percent chance of survival, Barb decided that she would be in the 40 percent. How's that for a positive attitude?

It is not only how she endured chemo for such a long period of time that made Barb a hero of mine. It is the way she lives her life today. As we celebrated her ten years in remission during the summer of 2008, Barb was both proud and humble. Her cancer experience has made her a different person in that she realizes more than ever how important family and friends are. She takes nothing for granted and thanks God each and every day for giving her a second chance.

Barb is also thankful to all those who donate blood. She had twelve transfusions.

Barb monitors her attitude. She has a pity party when she needs one but, for the most part, she understands the importance of self-acceptance and the importance of staying away from negative influences, regardless of how hard that might be. Cancer robbed Barb of some of her energy and she has accepted this. She has taught me how to do the same following my recurrence. I listen to her and I often take her advice when I am feeling low. Barb and I have our own box of secrets that we share with each other and no one else. We share a connection that is beyond our cancer diagnosis. Certainly cancer strengthened that connection.

You are probably wondering why Barb's story is in a chapter about writing a memoir. When Barb was recovering from cancer I decided that journalling her experience would be a great form of therapy for her. So I gave her a gift of a journal and encouraged her to "get busy" writing. It had worked for me so I was confident it would work for her. I gave her a second and a third journal before she finally convinced me that she does not keep a journal – and if she changes her mind she has three unused journals so thank you very much but no more journals please. I got the message. Not everyone likes to document their lives in this way.

However, if you do keep a journal and you would like to write your own memoir one day, this chapter is for you. I hope you find it helpful as you begin.

I journal every single day. I write about the events of the day, maybe something I am planning for the future or even something from my past that comes to mind on a particular day. By journalling each day I keep myself grounded. I put it down on paper, face it if I have not done so already and then I move on.

On occasion, I may include with the day's entry a clipping from the newspaper, an article that is of interest to me personally. This allows me to time stamp my journalling through a connection with what was happening around my world while not necessarily in my own world. You will be amazed how this all ties together years later when you are writing your memoir.

The single thing that worked best for me in terms of remembering details of my life's history was to take a separate journal and date each page with one year of my life. I call it my HBY – Highlights by Year. Some of our memories are triggered by other events that we hear about as we grow up.

When I was writing my memoir a few of my HBY entries read like this –

1946 – My birth and the year the *Bluenose* went down.

1947 – My sister Lois got her first pair of glasses.

1949 – Baths in the kitchen sink. No running water in our house.

1951 – Started school with the long walk to the Wilmot schoolhouse.

1952 – The TV test pattern and our first television in our Wilmot home. Only one other home in our neighbourhood had a television.

1953 – Swallowed a huge blue marble rather than share it with my sister.

1954 – President of the Junior Red Cross at school and the realization that I didn't like holding the position one little bit.

1955 – Moved to the big room for grades four to six in the Wilmot two-room schoolhouse.

1956 – Stuttering problem at school and at home and it was getting worse. Elvis was on *The Ed Sullivan Show*. My ultra thin legs seemed to be what everyone made fun of and it kept me awake at night.

1957 – I won marbles from all of my family and friends and began a collection that would fill a pillow case. (A skill that I hope I have retained and one that my grandson will appreciate.)

1958 – On the receiving end of a major beating from my father as he accused me of "crying and acting like a girl" after I cut my leg when a rock flew from our push-lawnmower. Mom had to insist he drive us to the hospital. I required seven stitches. On a more positive note, I met Princess Margaret during her train stop in Middleton that same year.

1959 – The day the music died with the deaths of Buddy Holly, Ritchie Valens and the Big Bopper. I began to excel in Middleton Regional High School sports and loved it – my high jumping skills became my personal "leap of faith." I experienced the beginning of channelling positive energy.

1960 – I won my second public speaking contest and loved the feeling of making eye contact with one person in the audience and then another.

1964 – Graduated from high school/left home/first job at the Bank of Nova Scotia in North Bay, Ontario, at the age of eighteen.

1965 – The first of my many big jobs at the Bell as I made a career change.

1966 – Met the man I would marry.

1967 – Married him.

1968 – Marriage rocky – this is not working.

1969 – Happy New Year – James Brian Scott is born on January 1 in North Bay, Ontario.

1970 – The Apollo 13 mission is called a "successful failure." My marriage could be described in the same way.

You get the picture. Many of these things were not direct memories, but by keeping a journal and noting some of these events even years later as I heard them mentioned it helped me immensely when writing my memoir. One memory often triggers another.

A memoir should include more than positive memories because life is made up of the positive and the not-so-positive. You need to ask yourself if you are prepared to share the negative experiences that form a part of who you have become. It is not always easy to add the uncomfortable truths to your story. Often you will upset members of your family and friends when all is said and done. Be sure you want to face the music when your book is published. Prior to publication, share the detail you have written with those who might take issue with it. It might soften the blow. In my case, it did and it did not. I sat down with my father to explain what I had written about him and while he drank it in he continued to badger me as only he could. In retrospect, he was better able to accept the negative impact he had had on my young life than some of his immediate family members. I was not expecting this and therefore not prepared for the negative onslaught that came from a few of the Cole clan. It definitely hurt and I wish I had seen it coming. Could I have handled it better? Maybe. Lesson learned.

Over the years I have filled literally dozens of journals and while writing this particular book I made a decision to pitch many of them. This is helpful to keep in mind if you want to journal but worry that one day others may read your negative thoughts. Once the journal has served a purpose for you there is no written rule that says it must be kept for future generations. For example, I don't think my son needs to read my personal feelings when I separated from his father. In fact, I don't need to read them either so that journal is gone. No one needs to read my rants at Bell Canada over the years either. My positive journalling about my Bell career far outweighs the negative but we all know it is the negative that some focus on when they read your words, so it is wise to be aware of what you leave for others to interpret.

Journals are meant to help you in the moment as you capture thoughts and memories you might someday want to re-read or share with others. It's very personal and often meant to be kept that way.

For me journalling is very therapeutic. For my friend Barb Harvey – not so much.

Holders of the Heart

*A*fter more than a dozen years the Comfort Heart Initiative continues to touch hearts – including mine. I receive letters that make me laugh and letters that bring a tear to my eye. I have said many times that this fundraiser is not about me. It's about those who have purchased or have been given a Comfort Heart. And it's about those who pass the idea on to others. With over 230,000 Comfort Hearts in the hands of Canadians and others around the world, this little pewter heart has taken on a life of its own. And it has raised well over a million dollars for cancer research. Each Comfort Heart sells for ten dollar with over six dollars going to cancer research.

Some Comfort Hearts have been purchased in bulk with thanks to Bell, Bell Aliant, Comtech, Shoppers Drug Mart, AIG, Canadian Auto Workers and other companies who have written a big cheque. The majority, though, have been purchased one at a time with a story to accompany each Comfort Heart. My thanks to each and every one of you too – thank you from the bottom of my heart.

You can order Comfort Hearts directly from OceanArt Pewter at 1-800-407-4436 or visit their website: www.oceanartpewter.com. Alternatively, you can contact the Canadian Breast Cancer Foundation Atlantic Region at www.cbcf.org/atlantic, the Canadian Cancer Society at www.cancer.ca, and you are always welcome to contact me at www.carolanncole.com.

The Comfort Heart Initiative is in memory of my mother, Mary Cole. Mom and I battled breast cancer in 1992. In January of that year we were both diagnosed, faced surgery and by month's end we were out of the hospital and discussing treatment options with our doctors and with our family. It was an experience that forever changed my life.

Over the years many different uses for the Comfort Heart have been shared with me.

1. Engrave and use as a gift tag on Valentine's Day – or any day.

2. Give to a special teacher or student.

3. Share as a token of friendship.

4. Offer the heart as comfort for someone who is ill.

5. Attach to an elegant cord and hang from a bottle of wine or wrap around a bunch of fresh flowers.

6. Leave a Comfort Heart under the pillow of a child who is expecting a visit from the tooth fairy.

7. Hang from a Christmas tree in celebration of the season or offer to others as a Christmas tree ornament in memory of a loved one.

8. Engrave to commemorate a special occasion – a graduation or wedding.

9. Mail with a greeting card to family or friends living overseas.

10. Give to a caregiver or as a token of comfort to someone who is undergoing treatment in the hospital.

11. Give a gift for your own mother on Mother's Day, or for someone who has been like a mother to you.

12. Wear a Comfort Heart on a chain or put it on your key chain.

13. Maybe even use as a ball marker on the golf course.

Companies purchase Comfort Hearts in bulk to give in recognition of employee service or to customers as thanks for their service. They are also used as prizes at company events and as employee gifts at Christmas.

I have received literally hundreds, if not thousands, of letters from people I call Holders of the Heart. Their personal comments speak to the true heart of the initiative.

"I am ordering these Comfort Hearts for myself and my family in loving memory of my Aunt Rose ... wearing this heart will forever keep her close to our hearts."

"My psychiatrist read about your fundraiser ... she gave me a Comfort Heart and I find it very comforting and soothing in anxious moments."

"I am in prison and there is little I can do ... your fundraiser sounds like just the thing for me."

"My wife carried a worry stone for years so I know she would like your Comfort Heart."

"My son is a haemophiliac. He received tainted blood in the late '80s. It is so hard for a mother to watch ... your Comfort Heart has given me something to hold on to."

"My friend Joan's baby sister, age forty-five, passed away being positive holding her Comfort Heart in her right hand ... till the end ... this little heart offers comfort to more people than you know. Debbie lived for only three weeks following her diagnosis."

"Thank you for the Comfort Heart in memory of my wife. With the cheque I am enclosing, please give Comfort Hearts to some people who can't afford them."

"I used Comfort Hearts instead of flowers when a friend's dad died. I took a heart to all of the children as well as the grand-daughters."

"I am a nervous passenger when flying so I always wear my Comfort Heart. I have never had cancer and wanted to let you know this heart works for me too. It's about more than cancer."

"The Comfort Heart is a subtle, gentle reminder that hope exists. I think it is for everyone."

"I need ten more – I keep giving them away for all kinds of reasons."

"My mother survived cancer in 1956 when no one actually talked about it. My sisters and I want to have Comfort Hearts for us and for her as a silent reminder that we are always here for her."

"Hey I am getting married and I need a Comfort Heart – for comfort – please send me one quick!"

"I gave Comfort Hearts to everyone in my wedding party and we engraved them with our names and the date. They were very well-received."

"My Comfort Heart comes with me for every treatment. Thank you and thanks to OceanArt Pewter too."

"I need twenty-five hearts – fast. And this is my second order – first order was for twenty-eight."

"I use the Comfort Hearts often as gifts of love and they are well received."

"We use the Comfort Hearts at a local women's shelter and the women appreciate them more than you can imagine."

"My friends and I call ourselves the International Wearers of the Comfort Heart representing the Canadian, the British, the New Zealander, the Israeli and the Japanese. We love our Comfort Hearts. Thank you."

"I am a recovering alcoholic and your Comfort Heart has helped me regain my faith and self-confidence."

"I love the concept of the Comfort Heart. It is simple, meaningful and versatile."

"My sister who lives in Valdez, Alaska, has a Comfort Heart and now I need you to send some to Mitchell in South Dakota please."

"My husband may go to prison for an accident that he caused. I hold tight to my Comfort Heart and am grateful to have it. It gives me strength."

"One of the teachers in our school here in Kennebunk, Maine, has been diagnosed with cancer. We want to give her a Comfort Heart and we all want one as well. Enclosed is our cheque for thirty-nine Comfort Hearts – as soon as possible please."

"I work at the Cornell Medical Centre in New York City. A friend gave me a Comfort Heart and I like it so much that I am ordering three for friends."

"This is a wonderful symbol of comfort and hope but more important is that it raises funds for cancer research at the same time. That is why I am ordering five more Comfort Hearts."

"As a result of recent CAW/GM negotiations General Motors has agreed to pay for the purchase of seven hundred Comfort Hearts. Please send them as follows … with the invoice to GM."

"I like the Comfort Heart – I really wanted to share my feelings with someone who knows what I'm feeling so I appreciate being able to write to you each time I order Comfort Hearts. Thanks too for writing back to me when you fill my order."

"I keep ordering these hearts – I sent mine to George Michael in England. He won the best British male singer on Monday, February 24, 1997, but was unable to attend since he was at his mother's side until she died. I wanted him to have a Comfort Heart."

I received a very special note from Audrey Giffin Bateman on January 22, 2002. I knew Mrs. Bateman as Miss Giffin, the French teacher at Middleton Regional High School from 1959 to 1968. Long after we leave school it is nice to be acknowledged by our teachers. Audrey wrote to order Comfort Hearts: "I am enclosing a cheque for $100 to pay for ten Comfort Hearts. It will be easy to find people who will appreciate them. I had only planned to order three or four – then I kept thinking of others and decided I'd better have ten. May God continue to give you good health and many blessings."

Susan Aker wrote in November 1998 to say her husband Don was awaiting a lung transplant and a friend had given her a "unique and comforting" gift of a Comfort Heart. Susan wanted to purchase more so she could pass the idea on.

I met Christie Delaney in 1998 when she was employed at the Fenwick Shoppers Postal Outlet in Halifax and I was mailing out Comfort Hearts daily. Our conversations took place Monday through Friday and when she left to pursue her studies the most appropriate gift for me to give her seemed to be a Comfort Heart. In 2002 Christie wrote to tell me she was working in cancer research and kept her Comfort Heart close by. She wrote, "Most days cancer research feels like I'm taking one step forward and three steps back. People wonder why we aren't making faster progress, and then they are surprised when they find out how much it costs to do research, and how unpredictable it is. Therein lies the challenge. Thank you for your encouragement all those years ago."

People come and go in our lives and it is so easy to lose touch. Years later Christie shared some very sad and personal news. After a seven-year career she was laid off from her job in cancer research.

Grant funds had been hard to come by and her boss had been in some financial difficulty. Christie was five months pregnant at the time and chose to see this as an opportunity to "grow and find something new and challenging." When her son was stillborn at forty-two weeks she found herself deep in the grieving process. That is where I found her. "I am doing what I can to recover and I hope for a brighter future" is indicative of her positive attitude.

This time, I vowed to keep in touch and when I e-mailed Christie in the summer of 2009 she had positive news to share. "I am working for the National Research Council in the area of stroke research. I recently finished my first 5K race in the National Capital Race Weekend. And I am slowly working on a picture book about my experience of having a stillbirth. I would like to help other couples who might sadly have the same experience. Whether or not my book ever gets published is not really the point. It has been a healing experience for me. Survival of tragedy, whether losing a child or facing cancer, to me is all about the support you receive. I hope to have my book illustrated by an artist who lost her son fourteen years ago. She has helped me in ways that I will never be able to describe. Hopefully I can pay it forward for other mothers like us."

Susan Smandych wrote on July 22, 2008, "My name is Susan and I am a Canadian citizen currently living in the U.K. I've had one of your Comfort Hearts for a number of years. One of my friends saw mine the other day and asked about it so I referred her to your website. She and others here in the U.K. are very interested in getting their own Comfort Heart. Is there anyone in the U.K. that sells them yet?" Susan and I have subsequently shared many e-mails. She has received two orders of Comfort Hearts so far and I am sure we will be sending her more. Susan is one example of how we are spreading the word about this tiny pewter heart all over the world. And Susan has since been transferred to East Timor, a country in Southeast Asia, so I expect to be sending Comfort Hearts there very soon.

Patt MacDowell and her friends participate in the Campbellford, Ontario, Relay for Life with her team called "The Comfort Hearts." Patt's friend, Nan, gave her a Comfort Heart during her own cancer journey and her many friends supported her through her diagnosis and treatment of Stage 3 invasive ductal carcinoma. Diagnosed in

December 2006, Patt returned to work in October 2008 following che-motherapy, surgery and radiation. Her friends are her personal comfort hearts. During the event as Patt walked past a luminary bag that read, "I miss you Mum," she gave thanks that her son did not have to write those words on the luminary he placed for her.

In September 2008 Mary McCluskey wrote in a note to Cynthia Ward, "The heart from Carol Ann is especially treasured since in the years since she started there have been great strides in breast cancer [treatment] especially. Because of that there have also been many advances made in the administration of chemo for all other cancers, making the process much more palatable." Mary fought a brave and courageous battle with bone and lung cancer and died after a hard-fought four months. She chose to see her Comfort Heart as a positive reminder of so many things. This is my hope for every Holder of the Heart.

When the Comfort Heart Initiative began in 1996, all funds were given to the Canadian Cancer Society. In 2000, in addition to CCS, I began working with the Canadian Breast Cancer Foundation and other cancer-related organizations. Most of the Comfort Heart funds that I raise personally are deposited with the Atlantic Region of CBCF. That helps to keep me connected with home. With the introduction of the Atlantic Studentship Awards Program I have the luxury of knowing some of the individual reseachers who receive Comfort Heart funds.

The Studentship Awards Program was introduced to inspire and encourage an interest among undergraduate and graduate students in the field of breast cancer research in Atlantic Canada. CBCF may award up to twenty Studentship Awards each year. The award, worth $5,000, covers stipend support for the student for a maximum of fourteen weeks. The Carol Ann Cole Comfort Heart Studentship Award will be granted annually and is one in perpetuity. During my recovery from mastectomy surgery in 2008, I had lots of time to think about the future – with or without me in it – and it is hard to put into words how I feel knowing that this award will make a difference for years and years to come. It is exciting to know I will have the opportunity to meet or at least correspond with students receiving this award – to meet the person who may one day be part of the team that finds the cure.

I have had the pleasure of attending more cancer-related break-fast events, luncheons and dinners all wrapped around the cancer umbrella than I can count – or remember. I am asked to speak wearing my survivor hat and I am humbled to do so. Often, sometime after the event has passed and we have all moved on to our next task, a picture comes in the mail with a short note. The photo serves as a visual memory of all those I have had the absolute pleasure to meet during my cancer journey.

Mental Illness and Emotional Journeys

*M*y emotional journey is not all that different from the journey of many others, and yet it is totally different. No two recoveries from depression and other mental health illnesses take the same path. My intent is not to tell anyone what they should do on a personal level but to share what has worked for me and for others who have been so generous and shared their story with me. They have done so in the spirit of helping others. Only you can decide what works for you.

We once called cancer "the big C" rather than say the word aloud. We have brought cancer out of the closet, thank God. The big C is now Communication and the need to ensure that we are able to ask the questions we need answers to and also that we ask the right person. I keep a journal and record my questions and the corresponding answer. You can't expect yourself to absorb information in the midst of a cancer hit. Write important things down, and don't be afraid to ask a second pair of eyes to be part of your journey. Have an advocate beside you whenever you feel the need to take strength from someone close to you.

It is the emotional issues that we don't always bring up and therefore we don't always deal with things like depression as constructively as we could. We often have to ask for help first because even those closest to us may hesitate to ask if we are depressed or if we are suffering from a mental illness. We have to be willing to help ourselves and when that happens others are often able to help as well.

In 1992 I did not fear death, but in 2008 I did. I feared death, health in general, femininity, sexual attractiveness and I harboured a great fear of that damn stamp that many people seem to think survivors have in the centre of our forehead that says, "Diminished." That poor-Carol-Ann voice of others that I would face a second time in my life ticked me off and frightened me even more. How would I deal with it a second time? Do I have the strength and energy to face the negative energy and comments once more? Depression set in.

Emotionally I worried and stressed about so many things, even my fundraiser. It seems a small thing now but it was huge at the time. Would I have the energy to reply to every letter sent to me and how could I make others feel better when I was struggling to make myself feel better?

I stressed about the social side of my life. As soon as I came home from the hospital, friends wanted to visit, including some friends who had never been to my home. Why now? I experienced one of the physical changes that come with too much stress and depression – sleep disturbance. I would literally be awake the entire night. I dreaded going to bed.

How would I feel as a woman with only one breast? So many questions. In the world today it is all about breasts as a part of being feminine and beautiful. Breasts are everywhere – they sell cars, pop and everything in between. Before realizing, or perhaps before admitting, that I really did need professional help I tried sharing my feelings with a friend. This was a total disaster but in fairness to him, he is not trained to give the counsel I was seeking. His answer was for me to find a man who would accept me "this way" (meaning with only one breast) and to move on.

Not everyone would agree with the decision to seek professional help. Again, it's a very individual choice. When I revealed on national television that I was seeing a therapist, one of my loyal Bell supporters e-mailed his praise and criticism at the same time: "Saw you on television ... did you realize that with satellite an interview in Halifax can be seen across the country? I always considered you the one Bell female executive who has balls but after hearing you say you need to see a shrink I am not so sure. What were you thinking?" I took my time replying and decided to take the high road. I helped with his education relative to what therapy today might look like versus the cobweb image he appeared to have in his mind. He took it well and we have since spoken. There are no hard feelings.

I am a tell-all woman and that includes not hiding the fact that I have battled an ugly recurrence of breast cancer. Some individuals do not choose to share such personal health issues but it works for me. I have nothing to be ashamed of. The support that came my way after revealing such personal information was both needed and yet sometimes overwhelming. I have a very strong family around me and when it was time to shield me from others, my family stepped in. Letting others know what was going on in my life kept gossip to a minimum (Is she dying?) and it served as great therapy for me.

It is often the little things you can focus on that will keep you moving forward – simple things. Complementary therapy can come in the form of yoga and other forms of meditation. Don't let range of motion restrictions concern you initially. Rather, concentrate on breathing properly. Breathing properly has been an issue for me for as long as I have been exercising and that's a very long time. I couldn't even stretch for a number of weeks post-mastectomy, so when I finally pulled out my yoga mat I was not flexible at all. Give it time. Work on your mind and spirit as well as the much talked about core.

Gradually, and with the help of a therapist I began to better understand my emotional journey. I had to speak about my feelings openly if my therapist was going to help me. Initially I tried to diagnose myself and began one session with, "I don't think I am depressed." Over time I realized and accepted that decisions like this were best left to my therapist. It is a day-to-day journey. I walk the path more boldly now than I did a few months after surgery. Don't fear asking for help. I am not done yet. I still ask.

When I returned to work after my initial cancer experience in 1992, I soon realized that I really did not want to be there. I didn't know where I wanted to be but climbing the corporate ladder no longer held the same interest for me. After only a few months back on the job I was transferred from my beloved Installation and Repair to the company's Logistics department. I welcomed the change and all of the new faces that came with it.

We had met once before.

J.C. Legault coordinated a conference for my entire department at Bell and after the event I thought, "This man knows how to make things happen." He was working in Thunder Bay at the time and my office was in Toronto, so it didn't appear that our paths would cross on a daily basis. But I believe life puts us in each other's path for a reason.

A short time later we transferred J.C. to Toronto and the initial plan was that he would work directly with me. I remember his first day as if it were yesterday. He flew into my office, as much as any human can fly. He didn't sit and it didn't appear that he could. He began to speak and it seemed that he was telling me at least five stories in one. He had a plan to execute every exercise and with great precision. I hardly understood one word he uttered. He didn't pause to take a breath. I couldn't find a spot to interrupt, so I raised my hand and my voice and said, "J.C., did you forget to take your lithium this morning?" I was kidding.

J.C. looked me in the eye with a stare that I could not read. Softly he said, "You know?" My heart ached for this gentle man. I did not know. I was not trained in the field of whatever field you are in when you prescribe lithium. It was the beginning of a friendship and a powerful education for me. I so admire this man.

The following is J.C.'s story in his own words.

My story is about accepting having a mental illness and survival. I am a manic depressive – bipolar.

Having gone through three major psychotic episodes resulting in being admitted to a psychiatric hospital (in two cases the psychiatric ward of the hospital) and living daily with manic depression, survival and success for me is achieved through the combination of acceptance of my disease and a willingness to participate in whatever it takes to be well. The support and caring of family and friends, and continuing faith that God and my angels watch over me, helps me every single day.

Before being diagnosed and treated in 1991, I had been through several highs and lows. By the grace of God and the patience of my family, friends and co-workers have I continued to become successful as a father and an employee. A brief overview of my life (sixty years and counting) includes being the eldest of six children and being brought up in a military environment where my dad was a member of the armed forces. I spent grades nine and ten at a junior seminary (St. Mary's College, Brockville), where I excelled in school and was at the top of the class.

In the mid-60s, my dad was transferred to Ottawa, where I have my first memories of manic highs … without drugs. I left the seminary environment and tried to do it all. I went to school, took days away from school to play pool and chase girls, joined a rock band. Eventually it all caught up to me, and I was expelled from school.

My life started to change for the good again in 1967 after having met my future wife, Elaine. From then on, with her encouragement I completed my high school at night (grades eleven and twelve in one and one-half years) while working part-time as a bartender and school cleaner. Next I entered Algonquin College, where I graduated with honours in 1972 as an Engineering Associate. I eventually found employment at Bell Canada and later SNC Lavalin, where I obtained increasingly senior positions and transfers. My career took me from Ottawa, to Belleville, to Sudbury, two appointments in Saudi Arabia, and then Thunder Bay, Algeria and Toronto.

I retired in 2008 and feel that I have had the most rewarding career and encountered so many fine people along the way. Many of those like Diane, Carol Ann, Judy, Sam, Gilles and Elizabeth endured my bouts of highs and lows and they were my angels. They helped me recognize the signs of mania and depression by bringing it to my attention before I became worse. I am grateful to these angels who, although they were conscious of my periods of having to be admitted to psychiatric wards, accepted me back to work without question and took a chance on me in spite of my condition after three major episodes.

There will never be enough ways to thank my wife, Elaine, for believing in me, loving me and standing by me – especially through the horrors of my psychotic episodes. I have known this angel for over forty-one years and I continue to marvel at her strength. Elaine truly understands me and she accepts me unconditionally.

I have experienced the stages of mania and depression at several periods of my life, usually caused by either a major occurrence in my life or not being faithful to my prescribed medication. In my case, mood swings from mania to depression will occur quickly and frequently, where I can be on the manic side one day and very quickly change to depression.

Usually the degree to which I experience mania will subsequently produce a corresponding low.

For me, being manic will occur in three stages. 1. Mania: racing thoughts; having several projects and ideas come to me, causing me to lose concentration on any one in particular; additional energy; overly talkative and talking at a greater speed; waking up very early and wanting to get going on something; starting to be more religious than I am normally; imagining myself as being attractive, being very creative and being able to take on several tasks, which sometimes bother the people around me who try to keep up; a feeling of "money is no object." 2. Hypomania: all the symptoms of mania become increasingly obvious; I may begin to imagine occurrences, have visions or hear voices, may begin to see myself as larger than life, superhuman if not like Christ or capable of extraordinary actions. 3. Psychotic: completely out of control, imagining myself in another form; being out of touch with reality; living as in a dream; imagining people taking on different forms around me usually extremely frightening to me; needing to be restrained.

For me, depression will occur as well in a series of stages: 1. Depression: feeling down; no energy; barely making it through the day; a feeling of wanting to lie down and rest all the time; low self-esteem; procrastination; letting things slide or not being responsible; dwelling on past sins and bad decisions. 2. Deep depression: exaggerated symptoms of depression to the point that all I want to do is sleep; I look forward to the opportunity to escape and lie down; my self-esteem is very low; I do my work but every step is a major effort; I will communicate only when I have to. 3. Suicidal: at this stage only my faith and my caring for those who love me keep me from taking my life; I want only to sleep so that I do not have to face myself; I feel extremely low and worthless; I begin to even imagine and think of specific ways I could take my life; I have gone as far as to close my eyes while driving for several seconds, but have quickly stopped, knowing that in hurting myself I would hurt others. 4. Psychotic Depression: I mention this state, as I am sure that whenever I have been hospitalized due to being in a psychotic state, my feelings during that time can be either psychotic high or low while being completely out of control to the point of needing to be restrained.

One thing I have been good at is almost masking the extent of my depression from my wife and mother, who are always watching for signs.

In my work environment I have been able to mask my depression pretty well – from everyone except my angels.

I attribute some of my professional and personal successes to having been in the manic stage at several times of my life. These periods have caused me to take on and accept assignments I would normally have shunned. I have acted with boundless energy and without fear or doubt of my abilities. However, sometimes feeding my successes with compliments pushes my mania to higher and sometimes dangerous levels.

For example, while working with Bell in Thunder Bay I began to take on far greater responsibilities beyond the expectation of my job, which in itself was big enough. I was in charge of all Logistics (Real Estate, Automotive, warehousing (materiel) and Administrative Services) for the 807 area code. I led the Zero Waste campaign, bringing in the city of Thunder Bay and Thunder Bay Harbour Commission, which led to having me present the program on behalf of the city in California.

I took on various campaigns for mental health and became the Chairman of the Canadian Paraplegic Association, and I organized several major conferences for our department, which is how I eventually met Carol Ann. I was transferred to Toronto to work with her. (No one ever feels they work "for" Carol Ann – she makes us feel we work with her. This was very helpful to me.) This occurrence and having this honour to work for such a great person sent me to a higher level of mania. Luckily for me, Carol Ann somehow recognized and pointed out my unusual behavior (even though she was not yet aware of my illness) and this helped me to get back down to earth.

Throughout my bipolar state, I have developed and volunteered for far too many tasks, which sometimes becomes overbearing. This can drive me back to depression. Outside of my work I have been President of the Optimist Club, Deputy Grand Knight of the Knights of Columbus, and I am an amateur actor in a community troupe. My wife and I are responsible for French Cursillio in Ontario South (a religious retreat movement) and I am responsible for the 5:00 and 9:30 mass choir. I also belong to a local old-timer's rock and roll band. On top of all of that, I am a father to four fabulous children and grandfather to Mila, our first wonderful grandchild.

I always say that my father, at the time of his death, gave me the gift of being finally diagnosed with manic depression, which helped me acknowledge and gain control of my bipolar state. When my dad died in

Ottawa on November 1, 1991, I was in Thunder Bay. I left immediately for Ottawa and as the eldest sibling began to take over the preparations for his funeral, including organizing the mass and teaching the songs that we would sing together as a family choir at his funeral. Everyone was amazed at my boundless energy and strength throughout the period from his death to his interment at the end of November. I did not realize that I was in a state of mania, which developed to hypomania very quickly on a flight back from Ottawa to Thunder Bay on November 29.

By the time I reached home (only by the grace of God and angels did I make it) I was beginning a psychotic state to the point that my wife was in shock and did not recognize me or my behaviour. The next day was a gradual series of events which brought me closer and closer to breaking for the first time in my life into a totally psychotic behaviour. It was at my daughter's high school presentation that Saturday night that I imagined I was God's angel, the Archangel, and that I was chosen to fight Satan that night at the school before he would try to do unspeakable things to my daughter. To the shock of my friends and my wife, I began thrashing around so violently that they had to call 911. The police first thought I was high on drugs, and put me in restraints and had me sent to the hospital. I woke up the next morning in a ward reserved for the criminally and violently insane – literally in the proverbial white room with nothing else but a mattress on the floor.

I could go on for several pages about my experience in this place. On the good side, I was finally diagnosed as being manic depressive and after some understanding that I had a problem, I was convinced that I would get back to my family in a good state before Christmas, and that I would be back to work by mid-January. To get to that point, I needed to demonstrate to my nurses and doctors that I was gradually getting better, by proving I could move through six steps: 1. to get out of restraints and isolation; 2. to be allowed in the ward and to walk the corridor; 3. to be allowed to walk the corridors outside of the ward for fifteen minute intervals; 4. to be allowed to walk the hospital grounds and to be allowed to go home for a visit; 5. to be allowed to go home; 6. to be allowed to go back to work.

I did steps 1 through 5 in two weeks and by January 15 I was back to work. I invited our vice president, Diane Chabot, to join me in Thunder Bay, where I faced all thirty-five of my employees and told them my story. Later that evening I was appointed Chairman of the Northern Paraplegic Association.

My second psychotic episode snuck up on me in January 2001. I had been assigned to the Marketing Department of our company but I had no background in marketing. I had several assignments, mainly to pursue contracts with Bell Canada subsidiaries. One of my assignments was to go to Algeria with very little information and try to obtain an agreement with the management of the airport. After three trips to Algeria it seemed the contract was finally going to happen but for various reasons a conclusion seemed to be dragging. At the same time, while in Canada I would regularly travel from Montreal to Toronto every week, and I would also try to keep up with my extracurricular activities at home. While doing all of this travelling I became less faithful to my medication, sometimes forgetting to take my pills for days on end, and I was also drinking more alcohol than I should, which is not good when you are on meds.

Finally, one weekend after Christmas, I became very manic and by Sunday morning I was totally out of it, imagining things, hearing voices. Elaine called one of my best friends, and also our parish priest. When the priest came over, I brought him to the living room where we had still our Christmas nativity statues. I explained to him that the way the statues were positioned was giving me visions from God about the secrets of the world. As you can imagine, it wasn't long before Elaine convinced me to go with her and my friend to the Emergency ward of our local hospital. At the hospital, I remember spending a horrifying five hours in the waiting room. Every person I saw took on another form that was threatening to me. I was crying and trying to get away, and it took quite some time for the hospital staff to finally bring me to the crisis unit. It was decided finally that I should be admitted.

Once more I went through the steps of recovery. There are a couple of memorable events that took place. When I was first admitted they did place me in the isolation area but did not restrain me. In the middle of the night I woke up and started towards the lunch room but for some reason the night nurse did not stop me. In the lunch room I saw a newspaper, and I read the date: January 16, 2002. Still in a psychotic state, I imagined that I had been admitted on January 15, 2001, and they had kept me asleep all that time. I had missed a whole year of my life! I started screaming and throwing things in anger. It wasn't long before two burly security guards got hold of me, and I spent the rest of the night on an uncomfortable stretcher with arm and leg restraints. (I hate that.)

A funny story is that I requested a razor one morning as I had not shaved in a few days. They must have considered I was okay and gave me a cheap disposable razor. In the washroom, having shaving around my beard and moustache, I decided that it was time to remove the beard and moustache. Then I decided why not the eyebrows ... and then, what the heck, why not the hair? So as best I could and as far as I could I started to shave the hair from my head until the poor cheapo razor could do no more. You can imagine the reaction of the nurses and doctors. This event set me back a few recovery steps. Elaine almost fainted when she saw me. The next day she arrived back at the hospital with a friend who is a hairdresser. She completed the job with professionalism.

Outside of those episodes I was a model patient, volunteering for all group sessions and activities that came around, going to the chapel each day, and volunteering to read even though my medication made my mouth feel like I was trying to talk through a burnt potato. I even had Elaine bring my guitar so my son and daughter and I could give a few concerts. I organized a movie night, with popcorn for all who came. After two weeks I was back home again, and only two weeks after that I was back to work.

I was always scared when leaving the hospital because of what my friends and co-workers might think of me being a mental patient. I am so grateful to those who took the time to call, write or visit me. Gilles Hebert, my boss and good friend for many years, stayed in touch with Elaine throughout my recovery. And Judy and Carol Ann, who with my wife, my mother and my kids form my company of "angels." They came to our home in Whitby to visit me after my release. Carol Ann made me laugh out loud when she found the right words to say she wouldn't be asking for the name of my hairdresser anytime soon.

I am convinced that heredity is one of the contributing factors of manic depression, at least in my case. I remember the behaviours of both my father and my brother, who was killed July 1, 2007, in a motorcycle accident. I suspect they were bipolar, although neither of them was the type who would have proceeded to obtain diagnosis or treatment.

One of the most difficult and heartbreaking times for me was finding out one day that my son Carl was himself admitted to the psychiatric ward of the Ajax hospital and was diagnosed bipolar. I could not believe that I was passing this on to my only son. Carl has had his own personal bouts when he has been forced to deal with the disease. He is fortunate that he has a very understanding girlfriend and family who support him totally.

When I was admitted to the psychiatric ward a third and final time on May 17, 2005, it was Carl who recognized the symptoms and was able to accompany me and Elaine as I went through the admission process one more time. Carl's experience with his own illness helped him convince the Emergency Room doctors that I needed to be admitted right away. Because of Carl's help I was able to be treated once more and fully recovered in time to attend my daughter's wedding on June 25. I consider this a miracle.

Some of my nephews have been diagnosed as being bipolar. We handle it together.

I thank God every day for my wife, Elaine. Without her there is no way I would have survived these years with bipolar. Her support through some very, very tough times and her unconditional love in the midst of these difficult conditions has been my salvation. If it sounds like I am repeating myself about the help Elaine gives me – I am. I can't help myself.

I hope to be able to continue to expand and improve my writing of my personal story, even though only a brief portion might be useful for Carol Ann's book, so that I can provide a clearer picture to my family and to all who have to live with those of us who are bipolar.

Ipsos Reid has reported in the past that one in four Canadians say they suffer from depression and that 64 percent with depression do not let it be known at their workplaces. It would not be wise to share with a new boss that you experience both the highs of psychosis and the lows of depression. The stigma exists to be sure – the stigma associated with mental illness that suggests you simply are not qualified for the job, whatever the job might be.

I have exchanged letters with a wonderful woman who, each time she orders one more Comfort Heart, shares how she is winning her own war with mental illness. She gives it no other name and over the years her letters have become more positive. "Finally I have a boss who understands that working is as important to me as it is to someone who does not have a mental illness. I screw up sometimes but he knows I am trying the hardest I can and one day I will not screw up." She asked that I not give her name or share where she works, but she is going to proudly show her quotation to her boss. My hat is off to her boss as well. Real work experience is so important to all of us.

Use of the Internet and more open dialogue has expanded the understanding of what mental illness is. We understand now that it can be far more than depression. The mentally ill are finding pride in who they are and they speak about it to help themselves and to help others by educating those who are interested in learning more. Some have come out of what they call the "mad closet" and are demanding equal time. They want to be heard and make it clear their conditions do not preclude them from productive lives.

I have always been concerned when I read about women suffering from pre- and/or postpartum depression being locked up rather than hospitalized when they break the law. It's true, we have all read the stories about women breaking the law in the most horrific way – the murder of their children. They are sick – very sick and need to be hospitalized and helped.

While it has happened here in Canada too, a case in the U.S.A. that made international headlines involved Andrea Yates, who drowned her five young children in a bathtub in 2001. In her first trial she was found guilty of murder even though she was clearly psychotic. Thankfully, in a second trial Mrs. Yates was found not guilty by reason of insanity and was committed to a state mental hospital, where she will be held until she is no longer deemed a threat. If she had been convicted of murder, she would have faced life in prison. Cases like this capture my attention because, for me, it falls under injustice towards women and I feel a need to do something about it. Or, at least to try.

At Mount Sinai Hospital women who qualify are eligible for an initiative called the five-day, five-night program when they deliver their babies. New mothers stay in the hospital for five days after delivery, adjusting to life with their baby and getting some sleep. Any depression is closely monitored.

Do you remember when Lisa Nowak, the American astronaut, drove across the country to confront a woman she thought was taking her man away from her? She was thrown directly into the criminal justice system rather than into the health care system and in a nanosecond the media pounced on the details. Her story was comedy for everyone. Her face was seen worldwide and she became a public joke.

I can't imagine what all of that did to her and to her family. NASA said very quickly that they would reassess their screening process and weed out applicants with mental illnesses. No comment was made about how, or if, they would treat existing NASA members who have a mental illness. Not here. No way. I hope Lisa Nowak is in better health today. But if she is, that would not be news so we are unlikely to read about it.

A high school student shared with me, "My mother has bipolar" and he wrote about how difficult it made life for everyone at home. He worried that "her disease could be flowing through my veins" but he was also positive knowing everything, at the moment, seemed under control. He felt his life sucked at times, as he put it, but it was sort of all right at other times. The lesson I learned from this young man was that depression and any mental illness needs to be acknowledged and discussed with our youth. It is easy to forget that the young adults around us need to be part of the conversation. They see. They hear. And they hurt right along with us.

When actor Heath Ledger died on Academy Awards nomination day January 22, 2007, the world mourned. A pharmacology expert said an accidental overdose that killed Mr. Ledger could happen to anyone. A young man who had shared his personal story of depression with me when I met him at one of my speaking events wrote to me after this particular story received such attention. He ordered a Comfort Heart for a friend of a friend who had managed to visit a number of doctors trying to find the right medication for his serious depression. He had been bragging about all of the pills he had thanks to his three different doctors. Apparently, the media coverage of Ledger's death caused the friend to reflect on how dangerous this was and he had promised to start over with one doctor and one medication. The young man who wrote to me felt that a gift of a Comfort Heart might be a good start. He later wrote to admit that the friend he spoke of was really him and that he was doing better. He was taking responsibility for his actions, admitted he needed help and was well on his way. I love stories like his and I know he will be proud to see that his recovery is captured here.

I admit too that news coverage of sad and even depressing stories can and does sometimes help others to see a bit of themselves in the story. If it helps even one person do something to turn their life around, the article has been worth reading. Media coverage is not all bad.

I have visited women's shelters and have worked with women who have been in abusive situations and need help. Their depression is very real and it often shows clearly on their faces. I have also known three men who have been in abusive situations and I acknowledge abuse does not only happen to women. For now, though, my focus is on women. I worry that not enough is being done to protect abused women who are in situations and some are ending up dead. Sadly, I know women who could write an entire book about how abused they are and what they are going through at the hands of their own husbands.

My interest in mental illness began during my youth. I would hear snippets of information about the Nova Scotia Hospital in Dartmouth and was always curious. Over 150 years ago it was known as a lunatic asylum and as kids growing up we often made jokes about who might be there. "He belongs in the nut house" would bring a chorus of laughter as we discussed someone we didn't particularly like. Initially the facility didn't necessarily treat patients but merely held them there, sometimes for up to two years. More than once my mother would remind me that I should only speak of those things I knew about and before I made fun of a patient in this hospital, I should think about why they might be there and how I would feel if it was someone I loved who had been hospitalized.

The more we bring mental health issues into the open the more advancement we will see. If we talk about it and get involved, change will happen. Some particular health issues, such as depression and postpartum depression, are receiving more attention than they have in the past. It's a start.

My Nova Scotia Home

*I*f I knew then what I know now, I would have packed my pride for my hometown when I left home in June of 1964. And I would have spoken about it with greater ease over the years. At eighteen "home" is often a place to get away from. Age offers clarity and home becomes that one place you return to, at least in thought.

When I think about growing up in Wilmot, Nova Scotia, I think about freedom, a tremendous sense of freedom. We walked to school and when a storm cancelled school during the day, we walked home and played outside in the snow until our mother made us come inside. On Halloween we would trick or treat along the road through Wilmot from one end to the other with never a moment of fear. We played outside on early summer evenings, and all summer long, until dark with the neighbourhood kids. We were totally unsupervised during games of pick-up baseball, Red Rover, Hide and Seek and marbles. In the winter we cleared the snow from the ice in the meadow and laced up our skates to enjoy the ponds that were gifts when the Annapolis River overflowed.

We had wonderful neighbours and could disappear into their homes without hesitation. We knew that if we bullied or harmed anyone, word would get back to our mother or at school word would make its way to our teacher, Miss Burrell, and we would be punished. The world has changed since my youth. I am thankful to have the memories and very grateful to have grown up in the Annapolis Valley.

Growing up in such a small community we learned early in life that everyone (and I do mean everyone) knew our business. We learned that life is not fair. We were not born equal in ability or in opportunity. We didn't spend much time thinking about this. In our youth we might wonder aloud why someone had a television set and others did not, and as a teenager we might share dreams of attending university that would forever be a dream and not reality. We accepted our life's path without much discussion.

The definition of home changes as we age. When my mother entered the workforce, for employment reasons she moved to Halifax with my younger sisters. My annual vacation for many years took me, not to the Annapolis Valley, but to Halifax to be with family. Halifax became home. Over the years I have combined geography, personal history, family and friends to create that feeling of being "home." For me, the Atlantic Ocean plays a huge part in my decision.

By the time we reach the age of sixty many of us have lived in more homes than we can count, or at least lived at more addresses than we can count. Not every address feels like home and I am no exception. I have lived in Wilmot, Nova Scotia, North Bay, Kingston and Toronto, Ontario, followed by Montreal, Quebec, and back to Toronto all before my retirement from Bell in 1994. Then I moved back home to Halifax. Then I moved back to Toronto. With all of the additional relocations within many of the same cities I have moved a staggering seventeen times. Often, house moves are career related and can't be helped as we compete in that upwardly mobile setting. After my Bell career I kept moving and when I relocated to Halifax in 1996 I thought that was it. In fact, I said to whoever would listen that I had moved home and would never leave. Never say never. I returned to Toronto in 2007 to be closer to my son and his family.

I speak of home often and I cringe at each of the down-home jokes I hear. Admittedly, I have almost as many down-on-Toronto jokes in my hip pocket so I can hit back when someone slags my home province. In 2008, when Newfoundland became a "have" province and Ontario became a "have not" province, many friends suggested I had moved to the wrong province. Good one.

Toronto is sometimes called the city of strangers – no joke there. I am trying to change that one hello at a time. It is unfair to expect small-town friendliness in Toronto and I realize it is important to keep

Liz Whitney 1964.

My 1964 yearbook photo.

your guard up among strangers. Maybe if I let my guard down just a little bit others will do the same. Human contact can be as simple and as easy as a greeting in the elevator. We have to start somewhere.

I am a proud Middleton Regional High School graduate. *"Virtus – Veritas/*Truth and Virtue" is the MRHS motto and I carry it with me each day. Many of my teachers left a positive impression on me. Al Peppard, my physical education teacher throughout high school, taught me to speak the truth and to accept those truths that I could not change. He understood my troubled relationship with my father and he gave me positive things to focus on, like being a first-rate athlete and doing my best always.

Miss Whitney was my teacher during my last year at MRHS. She encouraged me to be true to myself and my confidence grew under her direction. I vividly remember having discussions with other students about how old she was as we stole glances at her while we were supposed to be perfecting our typing skills. We reconnected in 2006 when she joined me at a Dartmouth bookstore while I was doing a book signing for *Lessons Learned Upside the Head*. We had so much to talk about and so much to catch up on. We completely lost track of time and spent the entire afternoon together. I was reminded just by looking at Miss Whitney that we really are the same age. A three- or four-year age difference is reduced to nothing once you hit fifty … or sixty! Our pictures in the 1964 *The Loudspeaker* (the MRHS yearbook) clearly show how close we are in age. What were we thinking when we labelled her old? I share this particular memory when I have the opportunity to speak with school students today. A teacher's age does not dictate what you can learn under their watchful eye. I still call her Miss Whitney because it feels right; I do have her permission to call her Liz, though. And I continue to learn about truth and virtue from her.

The MRHS Enhancement Association was registered as a charity in 2003 with a mandate to fundraise for a new gym and music room. The existing music room had been condemned due to its potential to produce hearing loss. Students were also at a disadvantage as the school only had one elementary-sized gym. Not good enough so the fundraising began with the community solidly behind the effort. The process was a long one but the money was raised, the construction took place and in late 2009 an official opening of both the gym and the music room will take place with thanks given to all who have helped along the way. I recall fondly the community support when I attended MRHS. As a teenager I was more aware of the visual support of parents and friends when students were part of an event that required an audience – they always came.

I have a wonderful connection with home and community as a partner in Café Central located in Kentville, Nova Scotia. Five of us opened the café in 2001. Wes and I are the "away" partners with Linda, Heather and Carrie all living much closer to the café. Linda manages the café for us so she is truly hands-on. We couldn't do it without her. When I am home I love sitting in the café and watching people come and go. I know some of our customers while others are strangers. It warms my heart to hear, "That lunch was some good" as a customer wipes his mouth and heads back to work. I observe personal greetings, friendliness and a concern for neighbours. When a much loved regular customer passed away, many mourners were Café Central customers who had always looked for her friendly face as they entered the café. In Nova Scotia strangers often reach out and introduce themselves so you are not strangers for long. I have met many wonderful people over the years by reaching out and introducing myself. In Toronto – not so much, but it can happen.

During the ten-plus years that I had the pleasure of living in Halifax I was in good hands medically with Dr. Maureen White and my oncologist, Dr. Bruce Colwell. I was not quite yet at the five-years-cancer-free stage when I moved home so finding the right doctors was critical. I felt that I could speak totally openly with both of my doctors about anything and while they were, and are, incredibly busy, when it was time for my appointment they gave me the time I needed.

In 2008 when I had my recurrence I contacted Dr. Colwell because something was haunting me. I had had my routine mammogram at the Dickson Centre in January of 2007. Something abnormal was noted and I was called back in six months. The second mammogram confirmed "nothing to worry about." So I did not worry. My mistake? Was something missed in the results of those two mammograms?

Dr. Colwell and I were in touch via e-mail until all of my questions were answered. He asked for a copy of my Toronto pathology and mammography reports and he further studied my earlier mammography results in Halifax. He answered every question I had and he allowed me to have closure to all of my concerns.

Nova Scotia is fortunate to have Dr. Colwell as part of the Dickson Centre team. Officially, he is an Associate Professor, Department of Medicine at Dalhousie University, Program Director for the Medical Oncology Residency Training Program, and Co-Chair of the GI Cancer Site Team of the Q.E. II Cancer Program. He is also a good guy with very strong soft skills – he cares enough to keep in touch when a former patient needs him.

Maritimers have a wonderful easy way of reaching out to each other. After reading one of my books, Paulette Cuillerier e-mailed me to tell me how much we have in common. She grew up in Kentville, has survived breast cancer, left home at eighteen to find her own "big job" and experienced a failed marriage. She currently lives across the lake from my son and she too enjoys being a Nana. We share e-mails now with the same comfort we would if we had known each other all of our lives. It's the Maritime way.

In Nova Scotia when someone recognizes you on TV they track you down. I love that. I appeared on CTV's *Live at 5* with Starr Dobson and the next day Beryl MacRae e-mailed to reintroduce herself and say she watched the interview. We had met when I was on PEI and again later at a conference in Toronto. She made my day by telling me that at her teenage grandson had read my book on a trip to Florida and came home with questions comparing my experience to hers. They had a great discussion and Beryl took the time to share her grandson's comments with me. She offered that her local breast cancer support group would add me to their prayer line. I'll accept prayers any day.

Another cancer survivor wrote following the same interview to say she was encouraged to seek therapy after hearing me say I had done so. In typical Maritime fashion she outlined in detail why she felt she needed to speak with a therapist and closed by saying she had just made an appointment to do so. She didn't need much help from me at all – just a mention that I had reached out and a listening ear via the computer.

I met Karen Murphy after appearing on a Halifax television program, *Maritimes Today*, a number of years ago. She called the station while I was on air and spoke with such emotion and honesty that she had me in tears. I called her so we could continue the discussion later that day from home. Karen lives in Lower West Pubnico. I have a soft spot in my heart for everyone from that area. We have kept in touch and when I appeared at a local bookstore in Yarmouth she arrived before I did and brought her entire family along. I was there for a book signing and she kept me company. Book signings can be humbling and sometimes lonely so a familiar face when you arrive is a gift. Karen was diagnosed with MS in 2000 but you rarely find her talking about her own health issues. She tends to focus on others, particularly her family – her growing family. Karen is a very proud Nana too.

One of the most interesting Maritimers I know is Mark Cusack. I met Mark at the Université Sainte Anne during a summer French immersion program. I was a beginner and I believe Mark was in the advanced class. In any case, because we were not permitted to speak English at all during the program I did not get to know Mark very well. However, I received a thoughtful ten-page letter after my second book was published. The letter was handwritten while he leaned on an airport chair armrest waiting for his flight. Mark confided that his oldest brother had passed away in 1990 and while visiting him during his brother's last days they spoke through touch. "I'm sure he heard what I had to say. He could no longer speak but he could still squeeze my hand."

I love Mark's male perspective on many things and as I read his letter I could see clearly that more often than we know the male and female perspective are one and the same. Mark wrote that –

– soft skills are important and can often be in place by age ten.

– no amount of whacks-upside-the-head will change a mindset if one does not believe in soft skills.

– small things matter and often say the most about a person. These skills are not necessarily taught during MBA courses.

– sharing personal experiences can help others.

– how to listen and the importance of listening is what counts. Shut up and listen is good advice and I am glad you reminded me of that.

– all that positive crap is not necessarily what the dying want to hear. I wish I had read your book before sitting by the bedside of my dying brother.

– keeping in touch with family is more important than we often realize.

I treasure Mark's letter and each time I read it I can picture him roaring out of the university student parking lot on his motorcycle. Who says tough guys don't have heart?

On Christmas Day 2008 I received an e-mail from Mark. I had asked for his approval of what I had written about him for my book and his reply further supported my view that he has a wonderful and strong soft side. Mark wrote, "It is 0645 and I have the buzzard stuffed and in the oven. I am sitting down with a cup of coffee and the cat and dog curled up at my feet. I laughed when you mentioned tough guy when you wrote about me. I don't see myself that way. My bike is for the environment – part of my Kyoto commitment and therapy for me. Don't get me wrong. I don't think of myself as a wimp either – I only eat quiche if it is covered with horseradish sauce. It is the women I know who are truly tough. Thanks for the image, though. An environmental Easy Rider works for me."

Mark is Chief Engineer on the icebreaker *Louis S. St. Laurent*. More important, he is a husband, father, grandfather and friend of many. Attached to his Christmas Day e-mail were many pictures of his family. I like a man who has the confidence to share family pictures with his female friends.

I continue to be a member of VWBN – Valley Women's Business Network – even though I no longer live in Nova Scotia. I work with them via long distance when I can. I don't attend meetings unless I happen to be home at meeting time but reading about all of the good things my friends are doing within VWBN keeps me connected. And grounded.

It's the everydayness of Nova Scotia and its people that I love so much and truly miss.

Jane Doe

*S*ome of my friends and even a couple of family members have suggested that after cancer I have become softer. I have always had, and am proud of, my soft side, meaning that I try to care deeply and openly about others. I suspect it is true that in some situations I do care more now than I did before my breast cancer experiences. Maybe I am softer. That's okay.

Jane Doe's experience took place before my 1992 cancer battle albeit I did not meet this extraordinary woman until 1998 – many years after cancer. I have often asked myself if my cancer experience has made me more aware of all things happening around me. I think so. If I knew then what I know now I like to think I would have given more of my time, and certainly my voice, to women's issues. I can't rewrite my own history, but today I can encourage young women, and men too, to be more vocal when it is right to do so.

This could have happened to any woman.

As she tentatively approached the microphone I couldn't help think of the horrible act of violence that had been committed against her. This tiny wisp of a woman with a voice softer than a whisper asked if she could sit down to give her talk. She didn't think she could get through it standing up. You could see the total honesty in her face. Jane Doe was raped by the Toronto balcony rapist – Paul Callow – in 1986 and she was here to tell her story. She began by saying, "My name is not Jane Doe and I am happy to share my real name with you. All that I ask is that you not repeat it to anyone." I can almost guarantee that no one in that room has, to this day, betrayed her confidence. The Canadian Auto Workers Union invited Jane Doe to speak during the violence against women segment of their annual women's conference held in August 1998 at their Port Elgin conference centre.

This story hit home with me and with so many other women going about their lives while living alone. I didn't live far from the Wellesley and Sherbourne Streets area during the 1986 timeframe. The balcony rapist had raped five women, including Jane Doe, after climbing up to their balconies to gain entrance to their homes. All of these women were in the supposed safety of their own home.

Jane Doe decided to do something about this terrible injustice and I am so proud of her for stepping forward. She decided to take on the Toronto police force. Not an easy thing to do. She sued, and won a civil suit against the police for failing to warn her there was a serial rapist stalking her neighbourhood. What upset Jane Doe to the core was the fact that police had known about a serial rapist before her attack and did not issue a warning. When she met with investigating officers a few days after her attack she was told that she had been raped by a serial rapist, that she was in fact the fifth victim. All victims lived in second- and third-floor apartments. They had all been stalked and all had numerous identifiable factors including that they all lived within a six-block radius. The point Jane Doe tried to make with the police was, "If you had all this information, why not tell people?" She was left feeling the Toronto police's reason for not issuing a warning was because they felt women would become hysterical if a warning was issued. She was further told if that happened, the rapist would flee. The police needed women to help them catch the balcony rapist. Unbelievable.

On a personal level I remember being enraged by the Toronto police department's insensitivity when I learned that their cross-examiner referred to the Jane Doe rape as "non-violent" because the assaulter did not cut her with a knife. This man lived right in the neighbourhood with his wife and he had a regular job. Whatever the profile of a rapist, surely this was not it. To add insult to injury, the police called her rape a "good girl rape," meaning not too young, not too old, middle class, white and asleep in bed with the doors locked.

In July 1998 Jane Doe won her civil lawsuit against the Metropolitan Toronto Police force and was awarded $220,000. It was not about the money for this brave woman who dared to challenge the police force. It was about how society must find a way to change how these issues are dealt with. The trial set a precedent that changed how police services across Ontario approach sexual assault cases. Toronto's city auditor at the time said the Toronto police force needed more training to better handle sexual assault cases and released a report that included fifty-seven recommendations to the police board. Two years later the police chief at the time said he agreed fully or in part with fifty-five of the fifty-seven recommendations. He further said he would implement fifty-two of the fifty-five.

So many people have made life less than easy for Jane Doe since that horrible night all those years ago. She gave a powerful talk some years later during the YWCA's Week Without Violence campaign. When she said, "The legal system is not a safe place for a woman who has been raped, and women who choose to enter the system should know what tremendous pain they will be forced to endure," she was speaking from the heart and from her personal experience. Yet the media and so many others attacked her.

A police detective said she was "surprised, shocked and hurt" by Jane Doe's remarks. What upset me the most was when the police were actually quoted as saying, "… sexual predators such as Paul Bernardo would welcome Jane Doe's advice not to report sexual assault." The attack of words seriously frightened this brave woman and I could picture her as she said, "When my own mayor, police force and government come down on me like a sledgehammer, it hurts." She was reminding women to be strong with their decision to report a rape yet it was suggested that she was advocating something else.

After hearing Jane Doe speak at the CAW conference I travelled to Toronto and met up with a friend – who is, or was at the time, a police officer. I had spent a bit of time with this man and I felt I was beginning to know him well. He seemed to be intelligent, honest and a true believer in upholding the law. I saw a different side of him when I said I had just met Jane Doe and heard her tell her horrific story. He turned on me in a second and with a sneer on his face he leaned very close as if to frighten me as he shouted, "What were you doing with *her*?" He made it sound as if she had been the rapist, not the one raped. At that second, and just for a second, I had a glimpse of what she was up against. Our meal arrived but I was longer hungry. I called him "weak" and that enraged him. He tried to lean in even closer. I walked out of the restaurant and have never spoken with him again. He knows why.

In 2008 different faces fill some of the chairs occupied by the decision-makers during the time when Jane Doe was raped in 1986. I read with great interest an October 17, 2008, *Toronto Star* article with the headline, "Sex assault audit put off one year." The subtitle said, "Review of investigations postponed until next fall to allow police time to implement changes." The article said Toronto's city auditor had postponed a third review of how the Toronto police investigate sexual assaults. This gives the police more time to implement certain changes that are already in the works – "specifically changes to the way officers are trained to investigate sexual assaults and handle potential victims."

Jane Doe's response in the *Star* a week later registered her disappointment. "It broke my heart," she said. "It represents a tremendous loss for women in the city and for policing." While there are two sides to every story, clearly Jane Doe feels police remain in the dark. Rape stigmas are as strong as ever.

Jane Doe still can't use her real name because if she does, her identity becomes reduced to that of a rape victim. Everything else she works so hard to accomplish and contribute gets lost. Her case and her research that are part of the curriculum in universities across the country – lost. Her insightful analyses of the policing of sexual assault – lost. Coverage of her full-to-capacity lectures where she tells all in an attempt to help others – lost. She deserves so much more.

In many ways, my cancer experience seems like a walk in the park compared to Jane Doe's experience. I draw strength from women like her.

Half-Past Cancer

*W*hen *Lessons Learned Upside the Head* was published I received a considerable amount of feedback on my chapter called "When Someone You Love Has Cancer." This particular chapter had been helpful to readers and I was pleased to hear so many personal stories with examples of just how helpful it had been. A number of readers suggested additions and changes if I ever updated the chapter, and you will see many of your suggestions here.

Since my first diagnosis, and certainly confirmed by my second, I feel I am living at a time I call half-past cancer. Not quite in that dreaded cancer world, but not out of it either. Survivors can relate to the fear that comes with every lump, every bump, every skin discolouration and every callback for one more test. It is not a case of being negative or a hypochondriac. It is our reality. It is what it is.

These are the lessons I have learned from living it myself and from listening to the experiences of others. I still make mistakes but I learn as I go.

Take time to find the right words when the cancer cloud hangs over someone you love. With my breast cancer recurrence I listened carefully for the words that would come my way and, like the first time, while many made sure their words were positive, others could not wait to give me their advice – and it wasn't pretty. Almost without exception, this advice came from individuals who had not experienced cancer personally. Comments like, "I bet you are sorry you didn't get them to remove your breast the first time you had cancer" and "I hope you will make them give you chemotherapy this time. You probably should have had chemo the first time" told me a few things about the individuals delivering these cutting words. First, they did not know what they were talking about; second, they knew even less about my particular diagnosis; and third, they hadn't read this chapter in my last book or surely to God they would have chosen their words a bit more carefully! These comments came early in my recovery and I didn't want to spend my time dealing with negative energy so I saved these conversations with these individuals until I felt stronger. The conversations have since taken place and we remain friends. Humour helped me approach how I had been hurt or angry and without exception we all learned a bit from each other during the exchange. We laughed together, and yes, we cried too.

Since my mastectomy a friend has told me more than once that I look "normal." And there is an element of surprise in her voice when she says it. I suspect she means, "You look normal even though you only have one breast" but I haven't had the courage to actually sit down and talk with her about this. The first time she said it, she wrapped it up with other words: "You look great. I am so happy to see you looking happy and normal ... so normal." I said something in reply at the time, but I was hurt by her words and didn't explore it enough to let her know that it was perhaps a poor choice of words. Cancer is new to her and sometimes she speaks without thinking – not an excuse but a fact.

My friend Al Stiff found the right words – twice. He wrote to me following my first battle and sixteen years later he wrote again. This time he included a letter I had sent to him many years ago in case I had forgotten him. I had not. His letter was longer and he took the time to suggest I "get on with it. Your fight will inspire many many others and perhaps that is why you have been called upon once again. I want to have another shot at saying I knew she had it in her." Al ended his letter saying, "Look in the mirror, Carol Ann. There is a winner in there." His letter arrived as I was arriving home from the hospital and could not have been more timely.

There are no magic words to use. There is no right time to say what you feel or to ask what you need to know. I work on this everyday with all of the people I know who are living under the cancer umbrella. I don't always say the right thing and I pretty much always know when I have said the wrong thing. I try to make sure I don't repeat my mistakes. It is a work in progress for everyone. The main thing is to be aware of what you say and admit, to yourself if you can't admit it out loud, that maybe you could say it better the next time. And remember too that often silence is what is needed rather than any words at all. The quality of quiet is undervalued at times like this.

The need to *Listen – be quiet and listen* is a skill that applies to life in general, not only to the cancer world. When I faced breast cancer a second time I received calls from many women in the same situation. Most were great listeners and I often moved forward in my healing with their help and guidance. Some, though, were not listening at all – and to this day I cannot understand why anyone would call a cancer patient only days after surgery to ask, "How are you doing?" but then to immediately interrupt and tell their own story, including why their recurrence was far more serious than mine. To be frank, I didn't care about their history at that time and did a bit of interrupting myself to let them know I was having trouble helping them feel better at the moment. To see if I could shut them up, I would sometimes interject with a bit of humour, "Could we back up and make this about me for a bit longer?" It usually worked.

I have had people suggest that *Lose the negative energy* should be softened to *Lose the negative energy when it is appropriate to do so* and I agree. It is not realistic to think we can, or should, be positive all the time. Believe me, for the first few months of 2008 when I went from diagnosis to surgery to recovery I had many a negative thought. I had my own pity parties when I needed them, I felt sorry for myself when I wanted to and I allowed myself to revisit my own negative thoughts, so I could deal with them. Would this recurrence kill me? Why me? Is there a strike three ahead of me? These are all negative thoughts, but confronting them and dealing with them at the time is better than pushing them aside or under the rug, pretending they don't exist.

I have a different view on buying time now. It took a recurrence for me to see that to *Buy time when you have the opportunity to do so* is a good rule to follow and in my case it was pretty clear-cut – pun intended. I didn't have to have a mastectomy but having the mastectomy has, most likely, bought me more time in this world. I will take it – purchased or otherwise.

Understand the initial flurry of visits, phone calls and mail will end. When we hear that a loved one has been diagnosed with cancer, or when we hear of any terminal illness, we tend to rush to their side and hopefully make ourselves useful in some way. I sometimes think we do this as much for ourselves as for the patient. We need to give. We need to feel useful. We need to give back. All of this is good. However, equally as important is the timing of our attention to the loved one now living with cancer, or living as a survivor.

Feeling part of the real world, whatever that is, can be difficult when cancer slows you down or stops someone you love in their tracks. As a survivor, when I saw the world going on during the days immediately following my surgery I couldn't help but feel that everyone was moving on without me. I lost a couple of speaking engagements because the words "she has cancer again" had spread through the company I was to address and because the company did not want to have cancer at the podium, I was replaced. I get that – it happens – it makes me sad but I understand better the second time that it does happen. Corporations move too quickly sometimes and don't stop to evaluate what they are doing to the individual. I did not have cancer; it was gone. I was, and am, the same person I was when they first hired me to speak at their annual conference.

To give credit, and in case some recognize their company in my words, they did listen to me when I felt strong enough and well enough to talk with them about this. They hired me again and all was forgiven. I think they learned from the exchange and I feel good about that.

Often cancer survivors have to take the establishment on even though it should not be necessary. What helped me in dealing with all of this was that some of my friends did understand that some of the interest in me following my cancer had passed and they made sure they continued to be in my life. One corporate friend offered a listening ear when I wanted to discuss my feelings about how some were, once again, seeing me under the cancer cloud, and he helped me with my plan to revisit a job I had lost. He jokingly said I should split my speaker's fee with him but I explained that my first paycheque following cancer had been spent on shoes. I think he was joking …

Months after my 2008 surgery, a card arrived in the mail from Steve and Laurie Wheatley. In addition to the words printed in the card Laurie took the time to write a personal note. I know Steve from Bell and from the Bell hockey tournaments. I do not know Laurie quite as well, which made her personal comments even more meaningful. This card came at a time when I was not getting much mail, and I was not hearing from as many people as I had immediately following my surgery. A small thing maybe but a big thing for me on that day. In a survivor's world the small things count more than you can know.

Cancer is a great change agent. It shows who we are and sometimes we surprise ourselves. Life does not have to be as it was before. *Here's your cancer – keep the change* remains a good mantra for survivors. I feel so strongly that cancer can be viewed as a doorway rather than a death. I continue to walk through doorways that my mother opened for me and I continue to change as a result of it.

Cancer does not only change the life of the survivor. It will also change the lives of those around them. October 27, 2007, I received an e-mail from Tanya Maillet in Port Maitland, Nova Scotia. Her words speak volumes to the changes cancer can bring if you have an open mind and are willing to change. In part, Tanya's e-mail read –

"Easter weekend 2001 my mother was diagnosed with breast cancer and had a mastectomy at the age of forty-seven. Good Friday took on a whole new meaning in my family's life. Good because the surgery was over and the nodes were all negative. We then travelled down the chemo street where Mom and I spend the summer bald. I worked at the hospital on Pediatrics at the time, and had many people ask if I had lost the bet, referring to my bald head. They didn't know I had shaved my head in support of my mother and what she was going through.

"I quickly realized how people touched by cancer are so easy to help. Every little gesture is so appreciated. I heard many stories and met many people because of Mom's diagnosis. I was actually enjoying being around people with cancer and it was at that time I realized I would make a career move and work in the oncology unit of our hospital. Since then, each day that I go to work, every person that walks through my office doors has a cancer diagnosis. I see their smiles and I see how they deal with what they are going through …"

I contacted Tanya in the fall of 2008 for an update and was excited to read the first line of her reply: "Mom is seven years cancer free." Tanya lives near my favourite beach – Mavillette – and also near my favourite antique jewellery store, Jeanne's, owned by Jeanne Wellington. I hope to meet Tanya on one of my trips home.

When appropriate, say "I'm sorry." Say it. Mean it. Move on. You don't need to repeat the words or dwell on them if you are sincere with your apology. With age, I find that I am more willing now to forgive others and also to say I am sorry about things I may have done that have hurt others. For example, a woman of colour pointed out to me that she was hurt when she has listened to me speak over the years and I continue to refer to "black humour" in the cancer world. I was stunned to learn that some might misinterpret my intended use of the phrase. I had used the expression for years, meaning that as survivors we often say things to each other that are a bit dark, we make fun of ourselves with other survivors and we do things we would never do with someone who has not walked in our shoes. I apologized for making my friend feel badly and vowed to change the phrase to "dark humour," which I have done. Lesson learned.

Say "I love you" more often. Cancer seems to soften us up a bit. I think of it not as a soft heart, but a generous heart. There are many ways to share how you feel. Find what is most comfortable and work on it until it feels right.

Do not be an Internet junkie. I still feel strongly about this even though I used the Internet more with my recurrence than I had in 1992. I know more now than I did when I was first diagnosed and I also know a bit more this time about what to look for. I know the sites not to rely on. I found that routing information I pulled from the Internet to someone who may better understand it could be very helpful. Don't be afraid to share what you are reading with others. They can often see things you have missed.

An example of detail that might be helpful to someone diagnosed with cancer for the first time is a cancer update from Johns Hopkins: "Every person has cancer cells in the body. These cancer cells do not show up in standard tests until they have multiplied to a few billion. When a doctor tells you there are no more cancer cells in your body after treatment, it means the tests are unable to detect cancer cells because they have not reached the detectable size." Good to know and a reality check as well.

Johns Hopkins also reminds us that sugar, coffee, tea and chocolate should be avoided. Given that we already know what is on the list of things to avoid, I don't pass this information on to newly diagnosed cancer patients. They will add these things to their personal list of things to avoid if and when they make that decision for themselves. I am still working on adding them to my own list so I sympathize.

Be proactive when you want to help someone. A cancer survivor often can't even think of what they would like you to do to help them. They need you to think for them. My friend Kathy Service came to visit shortly after my birthday and she brought me the most wonderful birthday present – she filled my freezer and my fridge with food. Literally, she filled it with individual meals that I could take from the freezer and pop into the microwave. And she brought me butter tarts – dozens and dozens of them. I did not share even one of the butter tarts. I ate every single one. My friend Pat Legg also gave me a gift of many meals. She mailed a box of food (and books to read) so big and so heavy that Connie could hardly lift it. Connie and James waited on me more than I care to admit.

Lighten up and embrace laughter every chance you have. Cancer survivors will tell you that we tend to have very little patience for those who insist on sweating the small stuff. To be fair, we had that cancer hit upside the head which helped us identify those things that are important in life. Not everyone is so "lucky."

Live every day as if it was your last. Honestly, I mean that in a positive way. Don't put something off for another day. Do it when you want to do it. See people now, not later. Write that letter, or e-mail today. If you want to give a friend a gift, you don't have to wait until Christmas – give it now. Live in the moment.

Don't worry or beat yourself up when you feel you have said the wrong thing. Learn from each mistake and try again. Survivors will be proud of you if you simply say, "I don't know what to say" or "I am worried I might say something that will upset you." We get it.

S A M – Sarah, Amoena and Me

*Y*ear-end 2008 saw me bidding farewell to my cancer woes while young Sarah was being lined up for her own 2009 repeat cancer journey.

I first met Sarah in late 2006 at Café Central in Kentville, Nova Scotia. She had been to the library to check all things breast cancer following her first experience and when she Googled the words "breast cancer" one of the things that caught her eye was my first book. Thinking she recognized me at the café she quietly approached to say, "I don't normally do this. Are you Carol Ann Cole?" A friendship was born.

As Sarah shared her story with me I was immediately struck by how young she was to have battled this killer disease already. Sarah was forty at the time of her initial diagnosis and surgery in 2004. She was familiar with my fundraiser and I was happy to send her home with the Comfort Heart I had in my pocket – for her daughter Rachel – as well as a copy of my second book.

Sarah's cancer journey included trips from Kentville to Halifax for her radiation treatments. She and her husband Doug made the decision to bring their two children along on one of her treatment days so they could better understand what radiation treatments consist of and also so they could be part of her life on those days as well as every other day. At ages eleven and fourteen Rachel and Thomas were in for quite an education. Watching their mother lay silent and very still while the radiation technologists lined the machine up with the tattoos on her chest to ensure that the radiation beams would be 100 percent accurate was a mind-numbing experience. They were in the actual radiation room while preparations were finalized but had to leave, along with everyone but their mother, and watch through the window as the treatments began. Rachel would later journal for a school project that when she looked through the window her mother looked like she was dead – and she looked so very small under such a huge and cold machine. Rachel was extremely frightened, but both she and her brother were glad to have been included on this particular trip to the city. They felt very grown up and extremely proud of their mother.

In December 2007 Sarah sent a wonderful e-mail along with her Christmas wishes. Rachel and Thomas were growing up and doing all of the things teenagers do. I was pleased to hear that Sarah continued to enjoy her coffee at Café Central and in particular I was pleased to hear that she was doing well. Life goes on. Sarah wrote about her pleasure in working with an autistic student since the child was in Primary. Nine years later the student was off to high school, having accomplished so much. Sarah volunteers with the school and the school board. Family, job and community commitments keep this lady very busy.

As I began my free fall back into the cancer world in early 2008 Sarah and I continued to keep in touch. She remained well, with no recurrence of cancer. Like me, Sarah seems to constantly undergo tests of some sort. There is always something and while we are thrilled to be monitored so closely, every scare brings with it many sleepless nights. Only another cancer survivor truly understands the depth of our fright. Sarah's positive energy is catching when you are around her and I can feel it even in her e-mails.

I received many wonderful gifts following my recurrence and one of them was three beautiful lingerie sets from Voula Pantelis, General Manager of Amoena Canada. Following my mastectomy I had not considered ever again wearing anything like the lingerie I looked at as I opened my gift from Voula. With tears in my eyes, hope in my heart and an oh-so-strong desire to feel feminine once again I tried everything on.

The very next day I wore one of my new lingerie sets – champagne-coloured with tiny polka dots – to dinner with two women I am very close to. These are women I can trust and I wanted their feedback. (I was not quite ready yet to share my lingerie-clad body with a man ... nor would my son appreciate reading about it here!) I wore a denim jacket unbuttoned so that my camisole was front and centre, so to speak. Earlier as I was dressing my immediate thought was that the camisole might be a bit too low-cut in the front so I initially put a tank top over my bra, under my new camisole – too much stuff. Eventually I decided I could go without the shield of the tank top. During dinner I constantly tugged at the camisole to ensure it was in place. I worried that my scar might show. Each time I looked down to check the camisole, it was where it should be. Any problem was in my head. The loss of a breast can reduce a woman's self-confidence and I was experiencing exactly that. And it takes a lot to diminish my self-confidence.

Finally, during dessert (and after two cosmopolitans) I asked my friends Barb Harvey and Faith Deloughery if they had noticed my new camisole. They had and were very complimentary. Barb was quick to say, "Carol Ann, this is how you always dress." Her comment hit home and made me feel so good – it would be possible after all for me to find lingerie I could wear post-mastectomy and continue to dress as I always had.

Feeling a bit more comfortable, I took it a bit further. I pulled my camisole down just a touch so Barb and Faith could see my matching bra. Honestly, they could not tell which breast was missing. Faith gave me a hug and said, "You go, sexy girl." It was an emotional moment between friends who knew and understood what I had gone through both physically and emotionally. They cried with me. On a lighter note, perhaps I pulled my camisole down a bit too far and held it there longer than I realized. The gentleman two tables over seemed unsure why I was showing off my bra but was willing to give me his full attention. He smiled and raised his glass. That was my cue to tuck my bra back under my camisole and get on with dinner. We laughed through our tears. If he only knew ...

A few days later I wore my new raspberry-coloured lingerie set. No one could see the colour under my black top, but the colour was not what was important to me as I ventured out that day. I was wearing, for the first time since my mastectomy, one of my favourite body-hugging tops. Not once did I feel a need to tug at my bra or check to ensure the side that held my prosthesis was in place. Both my bra and my confidence were in place. I felt feminine and, more important, I felt like myself. I had not truly felt that way in terms of my sexuality since the day I had my mastectomy surgery some eight months earlier.

Voula gave me three lingerie sets. I decided that I wanted to share my gift and pay it forward; I would give the third lingerie set to another breast cancer survivor. The chocolate-coloured bra and pantie set was ultra sexy. I decided it was made for my friend Sarah. She needed a treat. When I made the decision to share this gift with her I didn't know how badly she would need it.

A mammogram in September 2008 alerted Sarah and her doctor to some changes in the same breast where her cancer had been originally. She was being scheduled for a core biopsy and an ultrasound. Sounded all too familiar to me. As I read her words my mind was saying, "Here you go again. Hang on tight, Sarah."

I e-mailed Sarah to tell her about the Amoena gift I would like to pass on to her. We made plans to meet at the café on December 19 at 4:15 p.m. I would be home for Christmas with my sisters and would spend a few days in Kentville first. Sarah was hopeful that all of her tests would be completed prior to Christmas and that she would remain cancer free. She was hopeful but deep down she felt, almost knew, that something was wrong.

On her birthday, December 16, Sarah kept an appointment with her doctor and received terrible news. She followed that by keeping a commitment she had made to help with preparations for the school Christmas dinner to feed over six hundred students and staff. Life does go on.

Two days later as I was about to board a plane in Toronto for my flight home I checked my e-mail. I had a note from Sarah. "So, the verdict is not good. The pathology on the lumpectomy done a couple of weeks ago showed the same cancer I had four years ago. My surgeon wants to take the breast (a good chance that I will have both breasts removed). I will also have a sentinel lymph node biopsy as well. My head is whirling – I did feel something like this was going to happen. I don't know why but I just knew. We will catch up on everything when I see you tomorrow. Looking forward to it – safe travels to Nova Scotia."

Shit. Sarah would be forty-five years old when she faced cancer again, the same age I was the first time. She is far too young to face such extensive surgery.

Our time together at the café covered so many things. We talked at length about my family and her family and what the Christmas season looked like for each of us. Eventually we talked about what Sarah was facing. Only she could make the tough decisions about whether or not to have her second breast removed. I feel strongly that a decision like this should not be influenced by others — support can be given simply by listening. I was not sure the time was right to give Sarah the new lingerie, but she was thrilled to have it and assured me the time was absolutely right. I had put her gift in one of the Christmas bags that my sister makes for us to use each year. No wrapping paper for Lois — gift bags all around. Sarah was bold enough to open her gift at the café and left with a promise to let me know if she liked it and if it fit properly.

The following day we met again at the café. Sarah slipped a thank you note in my purse and I read it during a quiet moment. "Thank you so much for the bra set. I have never had undies that looked so great and felt so wonderful on. This means so much to me. I so appreciate our talk yesterday. It has given me strength and hope and enthusiasm for my future. I will be able to wear this bra after my surgery and it feels good knowing I will have something pretty to wear when this is all said and done — something I won't have to worry about looking for right away. I love the colour and I love the details on the bra — I feel really good in it! Thank you so much for passing this gift on to me. And please thank Voula too."

A few days after Christmas I heard from Sarah. She met with her surgeon and a date was set. She would have a bilateral mastectomy and she would be placed on the waiting list for reconstruction. Ideally, Sarah would like to have reconstruction at the time of surgery but this is not possible — the waiting list is a long one in Nova Scotia as I suspect it is in other provinces. I replied immediately to say I would have made exactly the same decision if I had been in this position when I was first diagnosed at forty-five years of age. It was not my place to offer advice as she struggled to make the tough decision, but for sure it was my place to offer encouragement and support once her decision was made.

Not long after her surgery date Sarah wrote to share details. Her bilateral mastectomy surgery left her with over seventy staples and she would need time to get used to her new figure. Her friends, family and the school where she works all rallied around her and brought so much joy to her life at such a dark time.

By March, 2009, Sarah was back at work and had already met with a lady who makes and fits custom breast prosthesis. Kellie Hayes is the owner of Health Solutions Just for You and dealing with her had been very positive for Sarah. Fully healed and with full range of motion with both arms Sarah is getting on with things. The waiting list for reconstruction in Nova Scotia turns out to be roughly three years and she is on the list. In the interim, she is happy, healthy and moving forward.

Life After Bell

It is impossible for me to write another book without again referencing my Bell years. I find it easy to remember the people who were part of most of my waking hours for over twenty-seven years. At the very least, I fondly remember those who share similar values, dreams and hopes. I have written about some of my Bell friends in different chapters throughout this book and there are so many more.

On October 14, 2008, election day in Canada, after casting my vote I sat down with hundreds of letters I had collected in my Comfort Heart file. I was searching for one or two more letters that I might follow up for inclusion in this book. One letter in particular caught my eye – from Donna Jelly. We had worked together at Bell and connected again when cancer invaded her life. Donna wrote to me in 1999 to say that she had made many new friends who were cancer survivors. She was busy giving away Comfort Hearts as well. As I read her letter again after so many years I put it aside. She would be one person I would contact. Without knowing any of this, later that day my son called. "Do you remember Donna Jelly?" He had just voted in Barrie where Donna was the Deputy Returning Officer. When he gave his name Donna asked, "Is Carol Ann Cole your mother?" There were about eight polling stations at the school and Donna had been assigned to the station where James was to cast his vote.

Donna would later tell me she felt part of a jigsaw puzzle that day. Indeed. I asked her to journal her story.

I often heard Carol Ann's name as she kept rising to the top at Bell and when she shared the Robert Fulghum poem "All I really need to know I learned in Kindergarten" I understood that she would have an impact on my life. We were on the same page and I felt good about that. Our lessons and rules for living a good life are taught at a young age. If we truly learn at a tender age, these lessons will carry us through our lifetime.

During my career, my main tactic for survival was to listen to the people, both employees and customers, and to learn the job process. Voila! People want to be heard and will tell you everything, the good, the bad and the ugly if you just let them. It was then up to me to decide what to do with my new knowledge. Listening goes hand in hand with sales, another little revelation. When I realized how simple this was, the rest was history.

Handling executive complaints was another responsibility I had at Bell. People would call the vice-president's office with an unresolved complaint and it would be my job to come to a satisfactory conclusion for both the customer and Bell. This was almost always a significant challenge because by the time the customer called the VP's office he/she was usually very frustrated. I would do some checking at Bell's end and then call the customer and open with something like, "What have we done?" and give the customer an opportunity to talk or vent while I listened. Again, I believe people want to be heard and of course respected. Things can usually be settled, not always as the customer wishes but at least they knew that someone had listened and heard their point of view. I remember a woman that I had resolved something for had such faith in me that she called me at home on a Saturday night because she had a very severe headache and wondered if it could possibly be a stroke. The solution here was easy ... call 911. I continued to receive Christmas cards from Mrs. S for several years.

Over my thirty-one-plus years at Bell I had many different jobs and interacted with thousands of people. I learned that every job has an interesting aspect and everybody is basically the same. People want to do a good job, be listened to and respected and have a little fun along the way.

I retired from Bell in December 1997 and looked forward to travelling, gardening, cleaning out those dark recesses in my basement, decorating and caring for my home and so much more. Every day I would get up with a plan for the day, a routine just like when I worked. For the first several months it worked well. I was able to accomplish some tasks, recon-nect with some friends and even take a trip.

Unexpectedly my world changed forever.

In June, I was doing some yard work and I pruned a branch of a shrub. When it wouldn't give way, I gave it quite a tug, pulling it to-wards myself and hitting my right breast. Initially, the pain was intense and then subsided. I watched and felt it every day, waiting for the bruise to appear. Nothing. In a few days, I did notice a lump at the surface but still no bruising and thought I should see about this but really expected it to be nothing. On my fifty-first birthday I visited my family doctor. She agreed it was probably a post-trauma hematoma but we would watch it. I eventually had a mammogram and ultrasound and another follow-up ultrasound and then surgery to remove it. On February 2, 1999, I received a call from the surgeon, who had also doubted that it was anything more than a hematoma as a result of my zealous gardening. He wanted to see me the next day.

The surgeon advised me that I had infiltrating ductal carcinoma. Cancer. A second surgery would be necessary to get clear margins and re-move lymph nodes to determine if the cancer had left the site of the origi-nal tumour and spread within my body. I was fortunate to have a close friend who had recently watched a doctor from the Sloane Kettering Cancer Hospital in New York on Good Morning America. The doctor was discussing a fairly new procedure called Sentinel Lymph Node Biopsy (SLNB). My friends, Ann and Marianne, scoured the Internet for infor-mation regarding this procedure and weeded their way through it to deter-mine what was relevant. They also made numerous phone calls to Sloane Kettering and to hospitals in Canada that were doing the SLNB rather than the traditional axillary node dissection which often leaves breast can-cer survivors with a condition called lymphedema. I was fortunate enough to be able to travel to Sunnybrook for my second surgery to obtain clear margins and check my lymph nodes in a far less invasive way. I was also able to have my twenty-five sessions of radiation therapy at Sunnybrook rather than travel to Buffalo or Thunder Bay, as so many women had to do at this point in time.

It was during my radiation therapy that I began my first volunteer work with the Canadian Cancer Society. I drove from Barrie to Toronto every day for my brief fifteen-minute appointment. Often a friend would accompany me but often I did the drive by myself … trying to keep life as normal as possible for independent me. I contacted the Cancer Society to let them know I was driving and if anyone needed a ride, I'd be pleased to have the company. I drove my first patient while I was still having treatment and continue to this day to drive patients about once a week.

I felt the SLNB that I was able to have because my friends were so persistent in their research was something other women should know about and include as part of their decision-making if they were candidates who met the criteria. Thus, I became a volunteer with Cancer Connection (the Canadian Cancer Society) to offer peer support. I continued with this role for several years until I felt my information may not be as relevant as it was in the beginning. The peer support was good for me as well as the women currently experiencing what I had experienced a short time before.

One of my first patients was on a breast cancer survivor dragon boat team, "Cup-Sized" in Stratford, Ontario. Another patient was someone I had worked with at Bell years earlier. Yet another patient was running into red tape and I was able to give her some information and assistance that made a significant change for her. We have become friends and see each other at least once a year. She felt so positive about the support I was able to give her that she nominated me for Flare magazine's Volunteer of the Year. What an honour to know I had made such a difference to someone else. Again, listening played a key role in my ability to be a good peer support volunteer.

After the cancer diagnosis and treatment were behind me, I tried to return to a normal life but things would never really be the same again, and I learned over time that this would be my new normal and that was perfectly okay. I received support from Carol Ann during this process and used her Comfort Hearts to get the message out. Instead of flowers I have given Comfort Hearts to grieving families. It is something each person can keep in their pocket as a reminder of the person they have lost. I read Carol Ann's books and was inspired to get my life back and at the same time perhaps make a difference to others. If she could do it, so could I.

Now it was time to have some fun.

In the winter of 2003, I received a phone call from one of my associates from Bell who had been diagnosed with breast cancer after me. Nancy asked me if I'd be at all interested in joining her on a dragon boat team. Our local public library would be having a dragon boat festival in the summer as a fundraiser for the library or another charity. I grew up in Collingwood and spent my life in or on the water either swimming or *waterskiing so my answer was an immediate, "Yes." In fact, I had driven to Collingwood the previous summer to see the dragon boats. I was unable to be there for the festival but I did see the basic long boat and I was intrigued.*

In the years since Barrie's Ribbons of Hope first used broom sticks as paddles in a conference room at the library as our initial practices, we have participated in dragon boating events locally, nationally at both coasts (Vancouver and Dartmouth) and internationally in Australia. We have raised over $90,000 to support our local cancer centre. Through this new adventure, I have made many acquaintances and some new and wonderful friends. I keep busy with the team as their secretary and assist with fundraising as well as paddling my heart out.

I felt that cancer can be beaten. And indeed it can. But not by everyone and not all of the time. It came as a terrible shock to lose two team members a week apart in the spring of 2004. We had only just begun ... what was to follow? We have lost others, including our coach, and it is truly devastating. There is life after breast cancer but only if you survive it. Most women do.

I have lost two people who were very dear to me. My friend, Barbara, was diagnosed the same year as I was and we were introduced by a mutual friend. I spent a lot of time with Barb and especially so the last two months of her life. I went with her for her treatments and was with her every day during her time in the hospital. You get through something like this knowing you made life a little easier for someone. You remember the good days ... even if it is as simple as going to a movie, dinner, shopping or just simply a coffee at Tim's.

Mary Taylor is part of the ROSE (Rays of Sunshine Everywhere) Volunteers. She wrote saying that what I had written about paying it forward hit home with her as she suspected it did with many Bell pensioners. Mary shared the exciting things being done by the ROSE Volunteers, formerly known as Telephone Pioneers. In particular, Mary is proud of a project called Coffee to Kandahar, adopted in December 2006. Money is raised to purchase Tim Hortons gift certificates for Canadian Troops in Afghanistan. With the help and support of family members and community groups, more than $15,000 in gift certificates has been sent. When the troops return from patrol they are given a Tim's certificate and a message: "Your friends in Canada want to thank you and buy you a coffee." Mary is proud that this project has been embraced by pensioners, existing Bell employees and so many others – all paying it forward.

When cancer took the life of our friend Jack Fitzgerald I received a wonderful note from Mary. "We are devastated over the loss of our beloved Jack. His death was not something any of us expected. The ROSE Volunteers still want to continue with your Comfort Heart program so if you would like us to take over from Jack we would be pleased to help you. Jack leaves a very big pair of shoes to fill but we want to try."

Jack sold literally hundreds of Comfort Hearts and always had copies of my books available for Bell employees and pensioners. Jack's commitment lives on through his family as well as with Mary and her team.

There are so many examples of how the Bell connection remains very strong. Mary and everyone on her team offer an excellent example of that connection.

The older we get, it seems the more names we recognize in the obituary columns of our local newspapers. Some are gone far too soon.

January 26, 1994, when my retirement was announced at Bell, I received an e-mail (called IIS within Bell then) saying, "… seems like just yesterday we were bundling the kids up to Mary's nursery school in North Bay and heading to work at 22 McIntyre St West …" Pat Rouillard was a peer of mine in North Bay and our children went to the same nursery school. I often shared my guilt with Pat that my son was always the last to be picked up. I would turn the corner to the school and see James with his nose pressed up against the window with that "Where is my mom?" look on his face. When Pat arrived to pick her son up at day's end she would find James to reassure him that his mother was close by. For the most part, I was.

Pat was promoted to replace me when I was transferred from the North Bay office and she enjoyed a very successful career. She died tragically at a very young age and we still miss her. There is something beyond description within the Bell family that allows us to not only keep in touch with each other but also keep the positive memories of those we have lost.

Throughout my career, my fellow Bell employees and I would often share stories about our children. When our careers took us in different directions and then brought us back together again, the first question we asked of each other most often related to our kids. Through the years, hearts have soared with success stories and hearts have broken when we learn that someone from our Bell family has lost a child. A parent should never have to bury their child.

When I began my career with Bell in 1965 I wasn't saying "pension" to myself or even "career" when I think back. It was a job that grew into a career that grew into an opportunity to leave at forty-seven years of age and explore other things in life. I had already battled cancer once and told myself at the time that I did not want to be at the office if cancer came looking for me again.

I am a member of the Bell Pensioners' Group, a non-profit organization whose objective is to protect the interests of Bell retirees with regard to their pensions and benefits. Throughout their years of employment, Bell employees are made a promise. They are told that they will receive pension payments – well defined in advance – after they cease active employment with Bell. BPG calls this the "pension promise" and our chief focus is on the fulfillment of that promise. News stories carry reports of pension plans that are in trouble. The Government of Canada could change the rules that determine, among other things, the amount and timing of payments into federally regulated pension plans, including Bell Canada's pension plan.

Ma Bell, like so many other companies, has changed. Increased pressure to squeeze costs can make it difficult to appreciate and understand why some changes are even considered. It is important to pay attention. Working with BPG keeps me connected with what is happening with our pensions and gives me the pleasure of reconnecting on a more regular basis with other pensioners. Like seventy-seven-year-old Larry Newman and his wife Barb. All those years ago I did not realize that pensioners helping pensioners would be such a pleasure later in my life. The clarity that comes with age is evident when Bell retirees get together. I am not saying we know it all, but together we try to figure it out.

175

Many of us have learned valuable lessons from the teachings of Ma Bell and they stay with us long after we retire. They apply to all aspects of our lives, not just while we are at the office.

* Allow those on your team to work with you rather than for you.

* Remember that ego isolates you.

* Don't be a slave to the dollar. Money speaks many languages.

* Share your soft side. Show that you care.

* Listen. Manage both sound and silence.

* Learn something every day.

* Give back to your community. Share your time.

* Communicate openly.

* Understand that messing up happens.

* Lighten up.

* Never look down on others.

* Be honest. Intelligence goes hand in hand with honesty.

* Look forward – not back.

Perhaps Alexander Graham Bell said it best. "When one door closes, another opens; but we often look so long and so regretfully upon the closed door that we do not see the ones which open for us."

Jalen James Scott

I am a Nana and, to be perfectly honest, I am not always sure what to say about becoming one. Those who are grandparents already know how it feels and how it changes lives. Those who are not won't get it until it happens to them. Each grandparent changes in their own personal way and it shapes us for the rest of our lives.

If you are a grandparent you will know who The Wiggles are. If not, your time will come, believe me. Tracey invited me to join her, Jalen and about ten thousand others who excitedly attended a Wiggles concert in Toronto. They are kind of like The Beatles for kids. The Wiggles are made up of Anthony Fiend (in blue), Murray Cook (in red), Jeff Fatt (in purple) and Sam Moran (in yellow.) The show includes many characters, like Barney the purple dinosaur, and each time a new character appears on stage the children shout and clap until their little arms are too tired to clap any more. The Wiggles and the children are in motion from the second the first character comes on stage until they exit over an hour and a half later. Jalen, and all of the other kids, sang, danced, clapped and completed all of the hand movements led by The Wiggles. Jalen sobbed in his mother's arms when the concert was over. He did not want it to end.

At day's end with Jalen tucked in bed Tracey and I shared a glass of wine. Tracey suggested we call it a Wiggles and Wine day. I concur.

Memories with grandchildren can be created without spending a cent. When Jalen visits we have a routine involving warm clothes coming out of the dryer. I let him know I am about to take the clothes out and he sits down near me knowing the warm clothes will be poured into his lap. Jalen gets to experience that flannel fresh warmth that comes from the dryer as he buries his face in the clothes. He offers me a smile that I can tuck away for a day when smiles are harder to come by.

I am filling a time capsule for Jalen. I try to capture events happening in our lives as well as world news. After reading the November 5, 2008, newspaper I tucked it inside Jalen's time capsule. When his class studies Barack Obama's rise to the presidency of the United States Jalen will have an original paper to share with his classmates. I followed the U.S. race closely and very early on I became an Obama supporter – even purchasing an Obama t-shirt from an enthusiastic African Canadian selling them along the Southbound platform of the Toronto subway system days before the election. They were excited to be doing something to promote Obama. I asked if they had been involved at all in our recent Canadian election. The answer was a resounding "no" but they felt they would do so in the future. One young woman felt she could promote change and she wanted to help others hope.

I am often reminded to not make comparisons between generations, especially when I see how advanced our grandchildren are in so many ways. I marvel when I see Jalen at his computer. No doubt there will come a day when he is able to help me with mine.

When Jalen was very small I began journalling his expressions and the innocence of his stories. I will share all of them with him when he is older, if he is interested. I have my favourites.

"Nana, did you know I came out of Mummy's belly? I growed and growed and her shirt got too tight and the buttons popped off and I jumped out. Then I was three."

Jalen asked for a treat and I made the mistake of offering grapes. "Treats are treats, Nana, and grapes are grapes. Do you have treats for me? And I don't mean grapes."

As Jalen was coming out of the bathroom and I was going in, he paused to give me instructions as only a three-year-old could. "Nana, me and Dad stand up because we have a penis. You have to sit down because you have a vagina (pronounced be-china)."

Jalen at work.

When Jalen began to learn where everyone in his family lived he would proudly give the address of his home and the same for his uncles and aunts and for his Grandma and Papa. When it came to Nana's address Jalen proudly said, "Nana lives in elevator." We didn't correct him until he was almost four. It was too cute and so innocent. He loves to press the elevator buttons and strike up a conversation with anyone sharing the elevator ride with us. He has to live by condo rules when he visits and sometimes to a four-year-old who has a large home and a backyard, not being able to light a fire on the balcony to roast marshmallows doesn't seem quite right. We were enjoying a summer evening on the balcony when Jalen asked, "Can you get some kindling so we can light a fire out here please, Nana?" He eventually understood we could not do that but he didn't approve. Jalen also feels somewhat constricted in my condo. On a rainy day after playing on the living room floor for most of the afternoon he softly asked, "Nana, can you get another room for this condo please?"

All grandparents are different and I marvel at those who have the energy to spend days and days with their grandchildren. I am good for "two sleeps" and then Jalen has to go home because I am bone tired. I don't try to hide it or do things I cannot do. One-day visits are a gift!

Ann Menlove, Jalen's other grandmother, and I picked Jalen up from school one day when we had the gift of both being with him. En route to the car we asked what he had learned in school that day. Without skipping a beat he proudly shouted, "The day is Thursday. The weather is spitting rain." He then turned his head to the side and spent a few seconds spitting and enjoying every second of it. So did we.

The intersection at Yonge and Bloor in downtown Toronto is busy all the time. On a very cold winter day Jalen and I were waiting for our turn to cross the street. Jalen took that time to ensure I understood when we would be permitted to cross – clearly he knew the rules. As is often the case, a few people stepped on to the street before they should. Suddenly they heard, "Stop! Attention please. Attention everyone."

Picture a four-year-old shouting with both hands in the "Stop" or "Show me the hand" position and his head thrown back so he could see from under his hood. He did get everyone's attention and he continued. "You don't cross the street when the hand is red. You wait for the little walking man to light up – there you go – see, there is the little walking man now. Come on!" And off we went with Jalen leading the way. One young man who had made the mistake of crossing the street on the red hand heard Jalen's rant and waited for us on the other side of the street. "Hey there, little buddy, thanks for reminding me of the rules." He was dismissed with, "I am not Buddy. I am Jalen James Scott." Enough said.

From Sweet Sixteen to Sweeter Sixty

*A*ll things considered, my sixteenth year was pretty sweet. I work hard to remember the positive – it is doable. In spite of my difficulties with my father, I was surrounded by three wonderful sisters and a mother who was making sure I had the opportunity to succeed. Like so many mothers, she sacrificed for her children. My friends were good friends, I had a great boyfriend (even though he dumped me), my health was good and I had my entire life ahead of me. I have a library of memories covering the first sixty years of my life.

The clarity that comes with age reminds us that the forever young crowd is not so young after all. Newspapers capture the so-called celebrities as they celebrate birthdays and we celebrate too. "Life begins at sexty," according to Dolly Parton. Those who turned sixty in 2006 (including me) expect to make it to eighty so we have lots of living to do. We are aging in every way. We exercise like we are under forty until boomeritis sets in and injuries plague us. The Terminator (Arnold Schwarzenegger) suffered a broken femur when he tripped over a ski pole – from a standing position – while out skiing. True, he was a young fifty-nine years of age at the time but he's proof that we do need to remember our age. If it can happen to him that easily it can happen to others. When Keith Richards fell out of the palm tree in 2006 while on holiday in Fiji and suffered a concussion, we were reminded that even as we age we are indeed playing hard. Too hard?

Indiana Jones said, "It's not the years, honey, it's the mileage" and he was right. We not only face injuries but we face disc problems, bad knees, shoulder rotator cuff tears and backs that go out, meaning we cannot. There is an expiry date on cartilage and as we age we only have so much left. Should we spend our cartilage over the years by running? I got over that years ago but not until I had done considerable damage. My knees ache just thinking about my days as a runner – picture me running up and back down the mountain in Montreal almost every day for the two years I worked there. I aged two years but my knees aged ten.

If there is an upside to all of this it is that once we acknowledge our mileage and what our body is telling us, we can, or should be able to, move forward and even get around better. I don't buy the "Sixty is the new fifty" or "Fifty is the new forty." Our age is exactly that – our age. Getting older sucks. It's as simple as that relative to aches and pains.

I exercise. I lift weights and work cardio into my daily life. Some days I go to the gym and some days I lie on my living room floor and call it my gym for an hour. Sit-ups have been a part of my daily ritual for as long as I can remember. Good results are harder to come by as I age but I stick with it. I constantly remind myself to keep moving and to move carefully. I have lost strength and flexibility in my muscles and tendons and I keep that in mind when I head to the gym. The good doctor tells me my bones are less dense (hate it when that happens) and more susceptible to breaks.

My full exercise routine consists of my own version of yoga, pilates and whatever else I feel like doing on a particular day. Exercise is not about vanity at this stage but about staying ahead of being a burden to our health care system long term. And it's about stretching. Lots of stretching. Stretching keeps me from having fix-me-itis, which often takes us older folks to the doctor with yet another body breakdown story. I sometimes try to be younger than my body but that's not working so well any more. It doesn't stop there – my eyesight is not what it once was and on and on and on. Secretly, I wish I had created the "Of all the things I've lost I miss my waist the most" bumper sticker because those words cross my mind each time I ponder just where my waist has gone ... and it's been gone for a very long time.

I met Dr. Kornelia Djetvai, chiropractor and acupuncturist, for the first time on March 2, 2001. A lower back injury, resulting in a foot-drop, was causing me considerable pain. I walked with a cane and was becoming more and more concerned each day that the cane might become a permanent part of my wardrobe. I had visited a variety of doctors and therapists and finally met Dr. Djetvai. She was the one who gave me results and relief after only six visits. I retired my cane. Living in Halifax at the time it was not easy to see Dr. Djetvai on a regular basis and, as is often the case, I neglected to book appointments to see her when I was in Toronto. Poor excuse.

During my 2008 recovery period I returned to Dr. Djetvai. It was time to take better control of my back issue and I was ready to make the required commitment. My visits went from three times a week to twice a week to once a week until we were able to get it to once or twice a month for maintenance.

I went to Dr. Djetvai with pain that medication was not helping. She took the time to determine exactly what was wrong and even more time working on those troubled spots until I had considerable relief. The first time she worked on me I almost cried in pain. Now, the treatments are actually soothing and I look forward to them.

I should have addressed this properly when the injury initially happened. Clarity sometimes comes a bit later than we would like.

Turning sixty caused me to reflect on comments my mother often made regarding how she felt about aging. For the most part, as always, she too was positive. However, she would tell me she was definitely treated differently once she reached sixty and not always in a positive way. Others saw right through her, not acknowledging her presence. She felt her opinion did not matter. She felt invisible. I didn't debate my mother's feelings because we had already agreed that everyone is entitled to their own feelings. I did tuck her comments away in the back of my mind (and in my diary) to be revisited when sixty invaded my world. Today, I wish my mother was with me still so I could tell her how I feel. I too sometimes feel invisible. While I understand what she was telling me I also wish I could have been more helpful to her at the time. I often dismissed her comments. I guess I was too busy. Or I thought I was.

Additionally, I wish my mother and I had talked more about whether or not she felt her body was betraying her over time. That discussion might have prepared me somewhat for the onslaught of health issues I am more and more familiar with now. In Mom's case, very different from my own, she did not exercise. I don't remember her even stretching until after her breast cancer surgery. Mom did eat well, though – three balanced meals a day and always something for dessert. She rarely had a snack in the evening but did allow herself a treat whenever she wanted one – which was seldom. Small portions were always served at Mom's home and James and I often shared a secret when we were invited for dinner. For a teenager, the meals were too small and before or after dinner James would need another one. It was our secret and one that I only shared with Mom many years later – she laughed too. My mother would not be a fan of the super-sized meals we see promoted today.

My generation views retirement much differently than our parents did. Today, some retire to travel, or to stay at home, to go to university, to do anything but work. For others, rather than retire we tend to move from one career to another and don't view it as retirement at all. When we choose a job that allows us to work from home we find ways to stay connected with others. For many, that connection is important. We are sometimes in a position to work less and play more and look for meaning and challenge in a second career. Because employees today tend to move from one company to another, it is possible for professionals with thirty years experience to work as consultants. The next generation needs this knowledge. Experience is vital to organizations and not always available in-house.

I knew who she was the instant I saw her and will forever remember the three questions she asked of me as we shook hands and introduced ourselves. "Tell me you are not a politician. I see at least one politician here and they should not even be considered for an award like this." I assured her I was not. "You didn't buy your award, did you? Money can't buy everything." And finally, "I trust you are wearing black because you like it and not because you were instructed to."

June Callwood and I were both at Rideau Hall on May 31, 2001. I was there to be invested into the Order of Canada and June would be promoted within the Order to Companion. Upon arrival the award recipients were separated from our family members who had accompanied us so that we could be given instructions as to how the ceremony and evening would unfold. When I entered the room, June was the only other female present (others soon joined in) and her lovely pastel-coloured shawl caught my eye immediately – no black for this lady.

As soon as I shared my passion for volunteer work and in particular my Comfort Heart Initiative, June smiled and we continued to chat on a personal level until others joined us. I was excited to tell her that my first book was coming out in a few months and we spoke about writing for a few wonderful minutes. I was actually encouraged to learn that this accomplished writer once had a fear of being rejected as a writer or of being seen as having written something that was not quite good enough. She invited me to contact her through Casey House and I wondered aloud if there might be something I could do to help. I said I would be in touch.

I am sorry to say that I did not make that contact. I have reflected on this a number of times. So often I refer to Charles Hanson Towne's poem "Around the Corner" when I am speaking with an audience. I remind them to keep in touch when they feel they a need to do so. The poem reminds us that if we keep putting it off we may be sad to learn that when we finally make contact it is too late.

> ... But tomorrow comes – and tomorrow goes
> And the distance between us grows and grows
> Around the corner – yet miles away
> Here's a telegram, sir. Jim died today.

When I read June's obituary in April 2007 I was first sad that we had lost such a wonderful, kind and powerful Canadian and then happy as I read about the gift her family had given her for her eightieth birthday in 2004 – a Mazda Miata.

We had more in common than the Order of Canada.

The only thing I have in common with Tupperware is that we were born in the same year. Earl S. Tupper, an aspiring inventor, introduced the product and a lady named Brownie Wise ran with it. Women didn't understand how to use Tupperware and she offered the clarity that was lacking. A single mother from Detroit, she sold Tupperware from a home-sales outfit and the rest is history. Ms. Wise persuaded Mr. Tupper to forget the supermarket sales and let her introduce sales through Tupperware parties.

By the early 1950s Ms. Wise became the face of Tupperware, certainly in the Florida area. My friend Nancy Stoddart became that face in parts of Nova Scotia when she moved to Sackville in 1971. With no vehicle and feeling that she was "stuck in the middle of nowhere at that time," she turned to Tupperware. Tupperware managers were assigned a car and this appealed to Nancy. She had small children and wanted to work from home. It was as simple as that and she set out to make it succeed.

To begin, Nancy had to have a home party and purchase the standard Tupperware kit full of supplies (a very large suitcase that would not meet the carry-on standards with airlines today). Her first party was a success with a number of friends booking parties of their own in addition to making purchases at Nancy's party. Her little business was going well.

Home parties were the only way you could purchase the much sought-after storage bins. Nancy jokingly says today that she was threatened within an inch of her life to *not* sell anything to anyone unless they held their own home party. The rules were stiff. As a manager she had to hold a minimum of five parties per week, have at least ten recruits who would work with her and attend weekly meetings at the Dartmouth distributorship.

Distributorship parties were fun. The hype was evident – you sang and you yahooed when new products were introduced. Nancy was presented with a brand new Ford Grand Torino station wagon with a big bow wrapping it like a gift. She had her wheels within four months. She was a Tupperware manager and her career was off and running … make that off and selling.

It didn't stop there. Nancy attended a national Tupperware rally in Toronto and not only did she receive the recruiter of the year award, but she also saw her first streaker.

Those who know Nancy would never call her shy, yet she credits her Tupperware career for helping her overcome her shyness. For her first party she made cue cards with a bit of information about the pieces she would demonstrate on each of the cards. As she was about to begin she dropped the cards and had to wing it. Her shyness was instantly a thing of the past as she flew by the seat of her pants and realized she could do it all. Opportunity can be found in a piece of Tupperware.

Often, we are well-equipped to speak to those things we have not done so well in our past. Failure makes a good teacher. Unlike Nancy Stoddart, I did not have a good work/life balance during my VP days at Bell. In fact, I had no balance at all – it was all work all the time. I was a proud workaholic. Today, more women and men seek a much better balance between work and home commitments. They are now more confident saying, "I want to spend more time working from home" or "I am leaving my corporate life to start my own business where I can be my own boss and set the rules as I see them."

Women don't necessarily rush out to buy balance by hiring more sitters or home care workers so they can stay at the office. Instead, they want to be part of that balance, which sometimes comes when one partner takes on the full-time job of family and home. That partner is husband or wife, not necessarily the wife. There are women who are at the top of their game professionally while their husbands have taken a wrong turn somewhere on the success at work road.

Gone are the days when the man was always the breadwinner with the woman looking after home and family. Gender no longer dictates who fills the role. To be fair, it is not always a case of the male not being able to play the game at work. Sometimes he elects to take himself out of the game and reinvents himself professionally while working from home and taking on more of the duties that all families face. It is a dilemma couples did not address decades ago. At the very least, they did not address it well.

Weekends are sometimes lost to the office. Some concede that weekend work has encroached on all parts of society, in all types of jobs. It is not only shift work and weekend rotation that is filling up the weekend hours but also the need to get a jump on Monday morning that finds many at the office on a Sunday. That was me beginning in the mid '80s. Sunday was always a get-ready-for-Monday day. My friends joked about not being able to spend any time with me on

Sunday because I was already thinking Monday. The joke was on me. Cancer was my priority-setting teacher. Just one way that cancer changed my life for the better. When I discuss this with some of my former Bell colleagues who saw my workaholic ways I sometimes say, "Thank God I had cancer." I am only partially kidding, to be honest.

Doing it all means something different to each of us. For those women wanting to break through the glass ceiling, even today all is not good. Early in 2007 executive recruiter Rosenzweig & Co. reported that the ceiling was cracking but not shattered: ninety-seven of one hundred chief executive officer positions were male, which meant only three were female. At a time when women made up more than half the population and 42.5 percent of the work force, 70 percent of companies were relying exclusively on male corporate officers to run the show, the report said. The old boys' network at the top of Corporate Canada remains alive and well. Sad to say even though I, and many women like me, felt we were pioneering the way in the late '70s and early '80s, not much has changed. Deborah Gillis, executive director of Catalyst Canada, confirmed this when she said, "The notion that we've shattered the glass ceiling is a myth."

The *Toronto Star* wrote that "women are still trailing" in a census detail published in May 2008. The report stated that in 2005 young women earned an average of $32,104 annually compared to $37,680 among men in the same bracket. Women's earnings did rise from 75 to 85 percent of men's earnings from 1980 to 2001, but then levelled off. This makes me angry. Admittedly, not the way cancer makes me angry, but angry in a not-everything-is-all-right-or-equal-or-fair way.

There are many different reactions to tears at the office. Today, if men cry they are showing their soft side and it's wonderful to see that men have come so far. If a woman cries, she must surely be up to something. Women continue to be encouraged to keep it together and to not appear too animated. They rein in emotions at work, even though male counterparts don't feel the same pressure to keep it under control.

I worked for years with men who would share their frustrations about "the wife" and rant in a totally negative way about their home situation. (To be fair, because I worked with many men, I want to make it clear that this only applied to a select few of them.) I did learn, from firsthand experience, that if I did the same thing it might end up in my annual performance review as a negative trait. If I had blamed what was considered to be unprofessional behaviour on my home-life pressures, I would have been seen as lacking in control. Did the double standard piss me off? It sure did. There is sometimes a fine line between what is considered traditionally feminine and masculine traits, and life has taught me that big girls do cry. What was once called a soft skill is now called emotional intelligence and is often part of a company hiring policy.

It's not about the tears. It is about being real, honest and not being afraid to put yourself out there. It's about bosses not promoting a double standard that says men can vent but a woman needs to keep everything under control. If I knew then what I know now I would have spoken up more than I did when the double standard was evident during the early days of my career.

Successful business men and business women have a very firm handshake. A firm and solid handshake during an interview is sometimes key to a successful interview. Research by Greg Stewart, an associate professor at the University of Iowa, found a direct correlation between how firm a person's handshake was and how likely he or she was considered to be a candidate worth hiring by a potential employer. People who present a good handshake tend to also be more extroverted. They likely introduce themselves better, carry on better conversations and use eye contact to their advantage.

I try to comment on the handshake when I meet young women just starting out in the workforce. It's a small thing that can be important and helping other women in this regard takes only a couple of seconds. In the early '70s when I met a new boss for the first time he commented immediately on my handshake. "You shake hands like a man" was a compliment to me and a lesson learned.

Women say "I'm sorry" far too often. We apologize when necessary and that's a good thing. However, we don't forget easily so we revisit the issue again and again with an apology each time. This dilutes the initial apology. We need to learn to say it – mean it – move on. In this case we can learn from the approach used by men. They apologize, move on and rarely think about it again.

Today, women are planning for their financial future better than ever before. You may hear it jokingly referred to as the bag lady syndrome. Women ask the question, "Have I saved enough for my retirement? What is in my bag, so to speak, for life after retirement?" There are countless financial planning seminars available to women and the experts giving the seminars are very often female. I like that. Women are finally looking at their financial future the same way that men have done for some time. And we speak about it openly, which is helpful for women.

Women supporting women has, for a very long time, been debatable. History would suggest that while we are celebrating Victoria Day each May we might not know that Queen Victoria was not all that supportive of her fellow females. In fact, she strongly opposed the right to vote for women. It was not until 1928 that British women aged twenty-one and older got the right to vote, ten years later than their Canadian sisters, and a whopping thirty-two years after the women of another Dominion, New Zealand, gained their political voice. For the vast majority of women in Canada and other Commonwealth nations, the legacy of Queen Victoria was social, political and economic repression. More than a century after her death women still do not have full political, social and economic equality with men. Clearly, women not supporting women began a very long time ago and today we must continue working on it. I still experience the sting of silence when I reach out to ask for help or guidance from some female executives that I have met over the last forty years and would consider friends of mine. Their silence is deafening.

In 2008, when Senator Hillary Rodham Clinton was covered by the media almost twenty-four hours a day in the U.S. Democratic presidential race, we heard over and over again that she looked tired, was gaining weight, had a bad hair day and showed emotion on cue. Her pantsuits became front-page news. Often, these comments came from women. Rarely did we mention her brilliant mind and outstanding career. I was struck by how many women took a personal negative stance against Hillary. They couldn't see her in the professional role – only as the female in the race who just didn't look right on any given day. Anyone, male or female, would take such personal criticism hard. I would. I would have loved to have made contact with Senator

Clinton but couldn't make it happen. I will keep trying. She has been busy.

Speaking with high school students one sunny spring day I was reminded of our vast age difference when one asked, "He's probably tons of years older than you but do you know who Conrad Black is?" I was able to tell them that, in fact, we are relatively the same age – Conrad Black might even be younger than I. These students were studying his trial in school and wondered what I could add to their education.

The first memory I shared went back to July 1992 when my mother was battling breast cancer and I was recovering from mine. Black married Barbara Amiel on July 21 and because my mother was interested in all news items she was able to brief me on the wedding news – his second, her fourth marriage. I had been in their company once at a Bell-sponsored function but we did not meet. They seemed to not see me, look right through me or look over me for someone more interesting. It was a feeling that would stay with me. I took great pleasure in telling the students that we had attended the same dinner in November 2005 to commemorate *Maclean's* magazine's one hundredth anniversary. At that dinner Black served (or his people did it for him) Peter C. Newman with a libel notice after Newman wrote that Black had been charged with violating U.S. racketeering laws. I didn't know this was happening at the time because they were seated in the front and I was at the very back. The message I offered was to look for the positive in life. The fact that I was in the back was not important. What was important was that I had been invited and I had a wonderful time. We discussed the guilt or innocence of Black but at some point the talk turned to my mother and the positive influence she had on my life. She would have been happy to know that on that particular day she upstaged Conrad Black.

When we discussed ways that students might feel good (or better) about themselves I asked them to reveal the first thing they would say to describe themselves. Sadly, many of the girls said, "I am too fat" or "I am not doing very well in school so I must be stupid" or "I will never get a boyfriend." The male students, on the other hand, are far more positive in describing themselves and seldom tackle their body image. The negative energy tends to follow the girls around and only by talking about it and bringing it clearly out into the open will we be able to change things and help young women feel more comfortable with who they are and what they have to contribute.

When I ask female students if they feel they are doing enough to support each other, I am often met with blank stares. By giving them examples of how I think women might have been more helpful to each other during my career it often opens the discussion about how they might help each other now. We are getting there and talking about it more and more will take us even further.

In 1997 I had the pleasure of speaking at a Famous 5 Foundation dinner in Calgary. The Foundation "inspires and educates Canadians to become nation builders in the legacy of the Famous 5." The Famous 5 are Emily G. Murphy, Henrietta Muir Edwards, Nellie McClung, Louise McKinney and Irene Parlby, who in 1927 launched the Persons Case. Believe it or not, back then women did not fit the legal definiton of a "person" and were denied the political and legal rights available to men. The 1929 court decision ruled that women were indeed persons and these five women changed the course of Canadian society forever.

The event was called Rising Stars and it brought together young women from the community, about five hundred young women approximately sixteen years of age. I encouraged these young women to stick around and speak with me personally if they wanted to. Shafeena Premji and her friends talked with me for some time, and Shafeena and I remain in contact today. A grade ten student, she was young, keen, and full of life with many goals and ambitions and hopes for her future. Shafeena spoke about wanting to make a difference in society one day.

Twelve years later, Shafeena is now in the medical class of 2010 at the University of Calgary and still finds many ways to give back as she continues her education. As a child she was deeply interested in the art of mendhi. Her mother had done mendhi on her hands for religious celebrations and in grade eleven Shafeena did mendhi for a bride for the first time – it took her six and a half hours.

Mendhi is the application of henna as a temporary form of skin decoration typically applied during special occasions like weddings and festivals. It is usually applied on the hands and feet where the colour will be the darkest because the skin contains higher levels of keratin, which binds temporarily to lawsone, the colorant of henna.

Over thirty brides a year currently enjoy Shafeena's mendhi art. She explained this love and passion:

"I find mendhi to be a type of meditation. When I work, all my stresses and worries disappear. I focus on my canvas – the body and skin – and let my imaginations and thoughts run free. I feel a deep sense of pleasure to be able to participate [in] and celebrate one of the key events in a person's life – their wedding day. The self-gratitude I get from making someone smile, helping them reach their wedding dreams and making someone look beautiful is a great feeling. I hope that despite everything that I do in my life, my mendhi will always be a part of who I am and something I can practice forever."

Having the opportunity to mentor Shafeena, even from a distance, is a joy.

A strong dose of reality comes when young school students give honest feedback after a presentation. These comments were written and given to me after I spoke with a delightful group of eleven- to fourteen-year-olds. I cherish every one of the notes I received.

"I am eleven years old and I liked your presentation. You are cool for an old person."

"I liked that you survived cancer but you don't think you are God."

"I am glad you talked about sad things like depression not only the happy stuff."

"Don't talk about Bell. My dad doesn't like Bell and he doesn't think you were ever a vice president either."

"I love how you talked about your son. It reminded us that you were young once."

"You teach stuff that is not on television. I mostly learn from television."

"I never thought about how important it is to listen. When you asked us if we ever felt like saying, 'Shut up and listen' when someone interrupts us I thought about my aunt who interrupts all the time."

"Your performance was rather cool. I didn't expect that when I saw you." Ouch!

"You made us feel important. Thank you for that."

"I learned it is nice to call people by their name. When you asked my name I thought I was in trouble, but then I saw that you just wanted to call me by my name. It felt good. And I wasn't in trouble."

"Mom and Dad tell some of the same stories you tell. I will listen to them now. They are old like you. I am eleven so I guess maybe you are just old to kids like me."

At one fairly large school I arrived early and observed many students, both male and female, smoking in the parking lot. I knew I wanted to talk about smoking and I tried to weigh my words carefully. One student asked, "Did you ever smoke?" and when I said I did not it seemed to work against me. "You can't understand then." It was a tense conversation and I left knowing I had lost the smoking debate.

I would be better prepared for the conversation today. Having had cancer a second time I am far more reluctant to spend too much time with smokers and inhale their second-hand smoke. Laura Wall is the Director, Southwestern Region, Ontario Division of the Canadian Cancer Society. We have worked together over the years and have carved out a wonderful friendship. In May 2009, I was Laura's guest at a CCS event and I asked her if it is true that second-hand smoke can cause cancer. She assured me that, unfortunately, the stats are true and she followed up with a quote for me to share. "What we know now is that second-hand smoke is dangerous and each year, more than 1,000 non-smoking Canadians die from the smoke of a burning cigarette, pipe or cigar. While children, pregnant women and older adults are particularly at risk, exposure to second-hand smoke for a long time increases everyone's chance of developing fatal heart problems, breathing problems and lung cancer."

Going forward, I hope to have many more opportunities to speak with students about a whole range of issues. When smoking is part of our discussion I will ask these young adults to consider those around them as they light up their next cigarette. There was a time when a clear decline in the smoking rate for young men and women was evident. Today, not so much – that decline has reached a plateau, which means they continue to smoke. Breaks my heart. If they don't want to quit smoking for themselves, perhaps they will do it to protect a loved one close by. This is one cause I will not give up on.

On June 15, 2008, I met Jillian McKelvey for the first time. We were both at the Toronto airport waiting for family to arrive – waiting and waiting. Lois was arriving from Grande Prairie, Alberta, to spend a month with me and Jillian's mother was arriving from Vancouver, B.C. Both flights were late and Jillian and I struck up a conversation. We were soon talking easily and sharing our summer plans. While my plan pretty much centred around recovering from my breast cancer surgery, Jillian's was far more exciting. She was off to Italy, from July 25 to September 15, to study Sex in Siena (aka Sex and Gender in the Italian Renaissance) as her final course for her Honours Bachelor of Arts.

Lois arrived and as we left the airport I asked Jillian to keep in touch. In particular, her mother had not yet arrived and I was worried for her but also I wanted to hear about her summer experience. Her mother arrived almost twenty-four hours later via Hamilton.

Jillian did keep in touch and in one e-mail she shared that for her final exam in Sex and Gender in the Italian Renaissance she wrote a paper on Rape in the Renaissance. This topic was from a course reader compiled by the professor to include articles on prostitution and rape. In Renaissance society you cannot rape someone who is no longer a virgin. Jillian had studied Women in Canadian History and wrote a book review on *The Story of Jane Doe*. "The patriarchal and misogynistic attitudes of men in the Renaissance and the hierarchical culture of male privilege which linked masculinity with virility and violence and commoditized female virginity could easily be Jane Doe exposing systemic gender prejudice in the Toronto police department, a department which perpetuated a rape mythology that treated women as objects – objects who must bear the blame, guilt and responsibility of rape." I found it interesting to read that Jillian's interest in the Jane Doe case was similar to my own – and I am sure to many other women.

Jillian returned home having had an "incredible, unique and privileged experience." She received an A- in the course.

One hundred and eighty twenty-something-year-olds attended the University of Toronto's Siena abroad program. In Jillian's class there were twenty-two studying Sex and Gender in the Renaissance – twenty twenty-year-olds, one thirty-year-old and one fifty-six-year-old – that would be Jillian.

I found Jillian's story to be a great reminder that age is a number – that's all. Additionally, because cancer had kept me close to home I was happy to read about her experience via e-mail.

Jillian's daughter gave her my book *Lessons Learned Upside the Head* as a Christmas gift in December 2008, and in reading it she observed that we do indeed have much in common. We have since met for lunch and have gone from strangers to friends, all because we introduced ourselves during a rainstorm at a crowded airport.

On Friday, October 26, 2007, I was the guest speaker at the Luncheon of Hope held at the Valhalla Inn in Thunder Bay, Ontario. These luncheons are a long-standing fundraiser in Thunder Bay with funds being directed to the new Thunder Bay Regional Health Sciences Foundation – Northern Cancer Fund for breast cancer research, patient care and support. I was honoured to be part of the event.

The audience was a very warm one, and Sandi Krasowski, photo journalist with *The Chronicle-Journal*, created memories by taking pictures during the event. As I raised my arm and shared with the audience that I was only a couple months away from celebrating sixteen years of being cancer free, everyone cheered and Sandi took a picture – the picture on the cover of this book. I call it my survivor shot. I later contacted Colin Bruce, publisher and general manager of *The Chronicle-Journal*, to ask for his permission to use the picture on the cover of *If I Knew Then What I Know Now*. He gave it to me – a gift. Good guy.

The Luncheon of Hope is special to me, not only because that is where the picture was taken but also because of the warmth of the audience. I often hear from audience members either directly after the event when we are all milling around or via e-mail (or snail mail) later. In this case it seemed that many of us had become instant friends. While I signed copies of *Lessons Learned Upside the Head* after the luncheon, people would tell me specifically what they had taken from my talk and how they would use it. "I like your idea that every job is a big job. I already feel better about myself." Or "You're right about people interrupting all the time – I do that and I am worried that you were talking directly to me."

I still hear from women I met that day. They tell me how they are doing and I tell them what is going on in my world. Some heard about my recurrence and sent cards and e-mails my way. I have family in Thunder Bay – my cousin Gary, his wife Lanis and their children Lindsey and Kyle so I was able to visit with them as well. I met their neighbours Bev and Dan Priestley and even though we only met that one day, when they heard of my recurrence I received a gift from them. Bev and I have since been in touch not only about my recurrence but about her breast cancer recurrence as well. Bev's e-mails are optimistic. In December 2008 she found a positive way to translate the details of her pathology report. "I had fairly good news. Only three of the nine lymph nodes were cancerous. First time it was eight out of nine. Plus, all margins were clear so Dr. Gehman feels he got the entire large tumour. I start chemo one more time in the new year …"

Great people live in Thunder Bay. It's an amazing community that rallies behind the needs of their own. I first met Bridgette Parker, Senior Development Officer, Northern Cancer Research Foundation when I was booked to speak at their event and we have since become friends. Northern Ontario has the highest incidence of breast cancer in Ontario. On the plus side, they also have one of the highest screening rates and survival rates in the province. Very proud people live in Thunder Bay and I can see why.

As what turned out to be my book cover photo was being taken, it did not cross my mind for one second that I would be unable to celebrate my sixteen years of being cancer free in January 2008 because cancer would come looking for me again that very month. I bet it didn't cross Bev's mind that she would face a recurrence either. Cancer does not send out advance notices.

In late 2008 I had another wonderful opportunity to meet and work with strong women. Virginia Nanouris is with a charitable organization called PEV – Promotion of Education and Values.

The mission of PEV is to foster the education of women of all ages and backgrounds in order to promote their unique influence in the shaping of society through their own family life, professional work and community action. The ultimate goal of PEV is to help women recognize the individual and valuable contribution they can and do make in society and to help them develop their talents to better serve others in whatever personal and professional path they have chosen.

PEV accomplishes their mission through the sponsorship of various activities. For example, their professional seminars and workshops offer activities for working women, which provide ongoing education in the skills needed to be competent and caring professionals. Emphasis is put on personal involvement as a key to enhance the workplace and to build relationships with colleagues and clients. Mutual respect, interdependence in achieving corporate goals, and work as a service and a means of forging character are fostered. Virginia contacted me to discuss my presentation "Soft Skills – It's About the People" and I was booked to speak at their fall seminar.

It appeared to me that many of Toronto's warmest women were in the audience. Not everyone in Toronto seems warm to someone from the east coast but this audience did and we shared a wonderful evening together. One woman approached me to say, "I love what you said about never saying things like 'It's just me' because, it's true, we are never just someone. I am a secretary and so often I say I am just a secretary – I will never say that again." During my talk I had mentioned that in my next book I hoped to write about depression and other mental issues and a soft-spoken woman stepped up to thank me – she works in the mental health field and wishes that more was said and done about these issues. They are often so hard to speak of.

Prior to turning sixty-five Lois asked if we could have a Nova Scotia sisters Christmas to end her big birthday year in 2008. Lorraine and Tom had been home the previous Christmas so they were with us online, on the phone and in spirit while Connie and I made sure that Lois had her Christmas "at home" in Nova Scotia. Lois arrived in Halifax first and spent a few days enjoying the city before arriving at Connie's new home in Mahone Bay. I caught up with them the following week. Even though we were up fairly early each morning, it seemed that lunchtime came with us still sitting around the table talking and sipping on Connie's lattes. She makes fabulous lattes. We did venture out but were always happy to come back home. As is our tradition we could not wait until December 25 to open presents and we began to give each other gifts almost as soon as we arrived home. Thinking alike as we so often do, many of the gifts we had purchased for each other were the same as those we received from each other. One exception – Lois made us aprons! Go figure – an apron for me?

Blizzards and much snow made for hazardous walking conditions, but as New Year's Eve approached we were determined to keep our reservation for dinner at the Innlet Café – a short walk but a long walk in a storm. The snow had not started when we walked to the restaurant. New Year's Eve is always important to me and this particular evening I wanted to thank Lois and Connie for coming to Toronto at different times to help me recover from surgery. Their help was beyond measure and I raised a glass in thanking them. It was time to put the year behind us – none too soon for me. After dinner, walking back home was somewhat difficult and not because of the wine. The blizzard had started while we had been enjoying the warmth of the café. Unlike me, both of my sisters had worn boots and could manage the snow well. My shoes were not all that suitable, but it was New Year's Eve after all and for me high heels were essential.

On January 1, in the midst of a snowstorm, Lois and I trudged through the snow to catch the bus to Halifax. I was wearing sensible winter boots that I had borrowed from our friend Shirley Allen. Connie helped us carry our six pieces of luggage and reminded us we would be on our own in Halifax. It crossed our minds that there might not be cabs available in Halifax and sure enough – no cabs at that end. We were now trying to manage the six pieces of luggage between two of us and remain standing as we attempted to walk in the blizzard. I have to admit that Lois managed far better than I. It might be because she lives in Grande Prairie, Alberta, and sees more blizzard-like weather than I do or it might be because she is in better shape. I kept stopping to take a break while she was eager to get to our destination.

We made the very slow walk along Terminal Road and on to a snow-covered Lower Water Street. We could almost see our hotel just past the Farmers' Market – not far. In the distance we observed a snowplow approaching. Thank God at least one side of the street would be a bit easier to walk on. A few minutes later the plow returned to clear the other side of the street. "Where are you gals headed? Are you okay to manage all that luggage?" came the question from the young driver. We explained we were halfway there and could make it, to which he replied, "Okay then, I'll clear the way for you. Follow me." He was off in the blizzard with his warm and caring Maritime manner. I miss Halifax! We made it to the hotel covered in snow and, at least in my case, gasping for breath. Lois was at the desk and checking in while I was still stumbling through the hotel front door.

The January 1 *Globe and Mail* said, "Nova Scotians prepared to welcome the new year with a dump of 30 centimetres of snow last night as a large winter storm swept toward the province." On January 2, 2009, *The Chronicle Herald* said, "Howling winds and lots of snow greeted Nova Scotians on the first day of 2009, as a record-setting blizzard knocked out power to thousands of homes and forced cancellation of flights." Picture Lois and me with those six pieces of luggage stumbling down the centre of Lower Water Street in the middle of the storm. Not pretty. Funny in retrospect, but not pretty.

A note I sent to the Halifax *Chronicle Herald* about our experience with the thoughtful snowplow driver was published and I received a trip-down-memory-lane note from my former physical education teacher at MRHS. "I am smiling as I visualize you and Lois high-stepping through the snow on Water Street. That instruction I forced on you (circa 1963-64) during hurdle training did come in handy. All the very best – Al Peppard." I continue to receive positive reinforcement from Mr. Peppard almost fifty years after first meeting him. He paved the way for me to think about myself in a positive way and I will be forever grateful.

We enjoyed every minute of our time in Halifax. We walked the boardwalk in rain, sleet, snow and sunshine. Connie came in to visit with us and we spent a wonderful afternoon with Mom's friends, "the sisters," who are now our friends as well.

The night before we left Halifax Lois and I sat in our room and, along with millions of other Canadians, we watched our Canadian World Junior Hockey team beat Sweden 5 to 1 to take the World Junior Title for the fifth time in a row. Next to the Leafs winning the Stanley Cup this would be the most exciting hockey to watch. I bet we were not the only grandmothers glued to the TV set that evening – no age barriers when it comes to supporting our teams. For me, our hockey teams in particular.

On departure day as we boarded the plane, Lois sat in first class (compliments of her employers, who own Curry's Jewellers 1978 Ltd.) while I made my way to seat 32A … think very back of the plane.

This trip was all about Lois and she deserved first class all the way. When Lois turned fifty our lives had just been torn apart with the death of our mother. Prior to Mom's death she had purchased a gift for Lois and it was one of the saddest days of my life as I watched her open that gift with tears pouring down her face. Not much focus was placed on her birthday that year because of our loss. We were happy to have had the chance to truly make a fuss over her when she turned sixty-five.

All was as it should be. Thankfully.

Those of us who have been around for a long time have seen it all – the 45-r.p.m. single, the TV dinner, the Pill, the bikini, the Volkswagen, the Walkman, the cell phone and the much talked about introduction of the latte, Viagra and BlackBerry. And the newer, if not improved, high-heeled shoes.

In our ever-changing world, there is more to come.

What I Know Now

Over six months had passed since biopsy results confirmed that the lump on my back was nothing to worry about. However, during those six months it did appear the lump had changed somewhat. In texture and in size it felt different so I talked with Dr. Tannenbaum about my concern when I saw him for my follow-up appointment. This was not a huge worry, but what I know now is that if it is a worry at all and there is a way to remove the worry, I will forge ahead in that direction. The lump had to go. My doctor was in total agreement.

At 8 a.m. on a bright May 20, 2009, I met my surgeon, Dr. Saul Mandelbaum. With him was a resident doctor at Mount Sinai who, although I did not confirm this, must surely be Doogie Howser, M.D.'s younger brother. Mount Sinai is a teaching hospital and I have always said, "Yes" to the question, "Are you okay with a resident doctor being in the room?" I chose to not catch his name because I wanted to call him Doogie Howser. Admittedly, I did not call him this to his face and I hope he will forgive me. For me, it brought lightness to the procedure and a smile to my face. Humour always helps me regardless of the situation.

I was face down on the surgical table, which did not offer an easy position from which to watch the procedure. The tumour was right beside my left shoulder blade and I listened carefully as the doctors discussed the incision. Specifically, they discussed the length and depth – would they have to cut into the muscle? I was hoping they weren't asking me that so I didn't speak up. Good thinking – they were talking with each other and definitely not to me. I continued to listen in on the discussion around removal of the tumour and the number of stitches required to patch me up and get me out of there. I asked to see the tumour. It was mine after all. It looked like a medium-size grape and I was happy to leave it behind. Me and my five stitches met up with my friend Laura who, once again, came to look after me. In this case, I didn't require lots of attention. We walked home, stopping for breakfast en route. Fresh air and food after surgery – always a good combination. By the time we finished breakfast, though, the freezing was leaving my back and I needed to go home. Another day in the life of a cancer survivor.

When I saw Dr. Tannenbaum two weeks later to have the stitches removed, I asked for a copy of the pathology report. The two most important words on the report were "grossly unremarkable." That is a medical way of saying, "No cancer. Get on with your life." I made an appointment to see Dr. Tannenbaum in six months for a regular checkup. That's it for now. Except for the appointment I have in two days with Dr. Leong, my breast cancer surgeon. Another regular checkup.

I seem to always be in the getaway-from-cancer car but I can't quite get away. I try and that's all I can do. My goal is to be cancer free for the next four forevers. That's what I know now.

My relationship with my son is as strong as ever, perhaps even stronger. We both have that clarity that comes with age and cancer. I pray that cancer never invades his world with Tracey and Jalen. Surely standing by his mother through it all is enough! We think back fondly on our younger years when we were growing up together. We lived well and given the current state of the economy we sometimes discuss whether or not we should have been spending so much money during the height of my career when we seemed to purchase literally anything we wanted. We have decided that we have absolutely no what ifs and no regrets. Regret gets us nowhere and revisiting yesterday doesn't work for either of us. I am incredibly proud of James. He has been an anchor for me, even when he was a boy, but so too have my relationships with my friends.

My bond with my female friends is more important than ever at this stage of my life. It is true that when all is said and done, your girlfriends will always be there for you. Women get together to share their joy, pain, success, love, loss, loneliness and everything else life throws their way. I may not always be a "best" friend, but I try. My male friends are important to me as well, and I have many. I know that I am fortunate to have been able to consistently prove that men and women *can* be just friends. I am truly grateful to all of my friends who have stuck with me through cancer and through clarity.

What I know now is that men of my generation are finding ways to show their soft side and are more comfortable with it. It surprises even them. Graydon Scott, my ex-husband, has been having health issues and in an e-mail he showed his. "I was talking to Jim last night. We took a trip down memory lane and talked about how, back in the '60s, four of us were called 'the monkeys.' It was a name that stuck. Two of the monkeys, Dave Sanderson and Bobby Garipey, both passed away at a young age. Jim didn't know I had been so ill and he was upset. It is amazing how men have changed. Before we hung up I said, 'Jim you are the best friend I have ever had and I love you and Beth.' I had to get off the phone after Jim replied, 'We love you too, Graydon.' It was very emotional." Jim Filipov and Graydon were best friends, air force police buddies and jocks when I met them in the mid '60s, a time when men were tough and that meant rarely showing your soft side.

At sixty I became a minimalist and for me it has been liberating. There is something cleansing about downsizing and I realized once I began the process that I had many things I simply did not need. I suspect that having had cancer influenced me somewhat – my priorities have shifted and changed so much – it is more about the person I am rather than what I own today. Downsizing is one step in the aging process where we can accept the loss of things once we learn to let go. I parted with some things that I had loved but was willing to share them and let someone else appreciate them as I had. For example, with the exception of my books by Nova Scotia authors, I found a home for my entire book collection.

I have met couples who have sold their home, purchased an RV and toured the world with all their possessions travelling right along with them. I have met others who feel better having downsized their homes and their lifestyles but were more comfortable enjoying their life in one location. Whatever works.

The act of downsizing was very therapeutic for me. No regrets when I think of the "stuff" I no longer have around me – with one exception. I can't seem to downsize my shoe collection.

Comfortable or not I have worn high heels from ages sixteen to sixty and beyond. In the summer of 2008 when flats were all the rage I actually bought and wore them. It's true, they were more comfortable. I couldn't say it, but others called them stylish. I purchased a bag to match one pair but that didn't ease the pain – the pain of not wearing the killer stilettos. Aging is inevitable but I can always open my closet doors and look at my oh-so-sexy-all-lined-up-and-yet-to-be-worn shoe collection. It has taken me decades to admit that my sexy shoes were, and still are, bad for my back and my feet too. There are some things in life we just don't want clarity on. Maybe my next book will be called *Lipsticked and High-heeled*. Or simply *Well-heeled*!

Honestly, if I knew then what I know now I would not change a thing. Well, maybe *one* cancer diagnosis was enough but I continue to learn about myself with every experience. Everything I have endured, the good and the bad, has made me the person I am today. My emotions and my body are battle-scarred in ways that I would have never imagined. I'm good with that, or at the very least, I am working hard to be good with that.

There's more to come. Hopefully, the Stanley Cup for the Toronto Maple Leafs and a cure for cancer – not in that order.

Until then, I would love to hear from you – wwwcarolanncole. com.